Walking with Prada

Our Journey of Love and Adventure

Silvia Mesa

First published by Ultimate World Publishing 2023
Copyright © 2023 Silvia Mesa

ISBN

Paperback: 978-1-922982-92-6
Ebook: 978-1-922982-93-3

Silvia Mesa has asserted her rights under the Copyright, Designs and Patents Act 1988 to be identified as the author of this work. The information in this book is based on the author's experiences and opinions. The publisher specifically disclaims responsibility for any adverse consequences which may result from use of the information contained herein. Permission to use information has been sought by the author. Any breaches will be rectified in further editions of the book.

All rights reserved. No part of this publication may be reproduced, stored in or introduced into a retrieval system, or transmitted in any form, or by any means (electronic, mechanical, photocopying, recording or otherwise) without the prior written permission of the author. Any person who does any unauthorised act in relation to this publication may be liable to criminal prosecution and civil claims for damages. Enquiries should be made through the publisher.

Cover design: Ultimate World Publishing
Layout and typesetting: Ultimate World Publishing
Editor: Maddie Johnson

Ultimate World Publishing
Diamond Creek,
Victoria Australia 3089
www.writeabook.com.au

Testimonials

"The face of a golden retriever feels like home."
David Rosenfelt

Prada.... How do I thank you?

You came gently into my world without even knowing and brought those beautiful babies with you.... Little did you know I was in the darkest place of my life. I had just lost my mom who was also my best friend, and I was failing at life miserably. It happened one day, I stumbled upon Prada's Bunch and Friends Facebook page and before I knew it, I was smiling, giggling and in time loving life. I would stalk your page to see their next adventure and before my very eyes I was healing. Your "Golden" heart, paws and soul had touched me in my darkest corners of my life and brought your loving, unassuming, gentle, and kind ways and shed light upon my life. Since then, you have brought me something greater than I ever knew possible.... Your human became a close and loving friend as well and now with your guiding spirit she is helping and touching other lives.

I will forever love you, Prada. XOXO.

Becky Potts
Ramsey, Minnesota

I have been a follower and fan of Prada's Bunch since the very beginning. It is a story of life from beginning to end with all the challenges in between. Throughout, it is filled with heartfelt inspirational stories of hope, faith, service, and encouragement. It is a story of love more than anything else. Thank you for letting me be a part of your incredible journey.

Glenda Alford
Stephenville, Texas

Our Journey of Love and Adventure

Mami Prada showed that when faced with challenges beyond our control, we can continue to live our best life and give to others. Prada's smile and pure heart brought joy to all who were graced with her presence whether in person or through the miles. She helped young children learn that having an illness or disability does not define who they are. Prada demonstrated that love heals and helps to fill the missing parts of our souls. Her smile, work, and dedication to working with adults and children taught us courage and that we can keep moving forward and living and sharing the best parts of ourselves.

Prada changed how kids view their disabilities. They believed that if Mami Prada could overcome cancer, then they could face their struggles with life as well. She helped young children learn that with love, patience, and kindness, they too could make a difference in the world regardless of their disability.

Carrie Lamberti
Flagstaff, Arizona

I am truly blessed to have been a part of Prada's journey. She was such a special girl. Prada always lit up the room with her presence and facial expressions. She truly had a unique smile and the cutest black spot on her tongue. She loved children and people from all walks of life. It is amazing how much love and laughter she brought into the lives of all who knew her. She will be missed forever. Her legacy lives on through her bunch who continue to show empathy and bring happiness and love to all they meet. They all truly make this world a better place.

Dr. Carmen Vazquez
Prada's Bunch Veterinarian
Miami, Florida

Prada's Bunch has truly touched so many hearts, bringing joy and healing wherever they go. Silvia has beautifully encapsulated their journey as a ray of sunshine, and they bring hope to so many. It has been inspiring watching them grow into gorgeous therapy dogs with a special life purpose. Reading about them always makes me smile. Thank you, Silvia, for sharing their adventures.

Wishing you every success with Walking with Prada.

Archana Mahtani
London U.K

I have a special place in my heart for Silvia, Prada, Charlie Brown, and Lalique. I met them several years ago and have seen how both adults and children are touched by the work they do. They have, and they share, love and compassion with everyone who meets them. Their work has helped not only people, but other canines as well. They never forgot the shelter dogs of Homestead, Florida. Their fundraising efforts throughout the years raised money for food and other much-needed essential items for our shelter. They also helped dogs get adopted. One event was a photo shoot at a dance studio with young dancers and rescue dogs. Every dog that participated in that photo shoot was adopted! Their work helped raise awareness of the plight of abandoned dogs.

Maria Elena Delange
Volunteer & Adoption Coordinator, Born Free Pet Shelter
Miami, Fl

Since the day I started following Prada and saw her give birth to her "bunch" she became an important part of my daily joy.

Danette Serr
Alberta, Canada

Our Journey of Love and Adventure

To know Silvia and Prada's Bunch is to know love, joy, kindness, and inspiration. It started as just sharing the antics and adventures of a mama golden retriever and her only litter of pups, and it became an inspiring adventure into the world of therapy dogs. Silvia has brought us along on the adventure as Mami Prada and the Bunch bring comfort to patients in a children's psych ward, smiles to residents of nursing homes, confidence to children learning to read, and love to so many others along their journey. They have been a blessing to my life, and I am privileged to call Silvia a dear friend.

Rebekah Santaw
Easley, South Carolina

I fell in love with Prada and Prada's Bunch online in March of 2015. I have followed their growth from tiny puppies to mischief seekers and adventure lovers to grown up dogs. Prada's Bunch posts have been the highlight of my every day. I have laughed and cried with them through holidays, illnesses, and family happenings, both theirs and my own. The magnitude of caring and praying for Prada during her cancer treatment was a testament to the friendships and the loving community of Golden Lovers that Silvia created by her posts. Her selfless generosity and mission through therapy is outstanding.

Sandee Aldrich
Marquette, Michigan

I am a Prada's Bunch fan from the very beginning of their adventure! Their adventure brings a smile to my face every single day. I cannot miss them! I am hooked! Not on the look but on Prada's Bunch adventures bringing joy and happiness!

Corine Philips
Knokke-Heist Belgium

I live in Chicago, and I discovered Silvia and Prada's Bunch almost nine years ago on Facebook. The Bunch included Prada (Mami), Charlie and Lalique, which are golden retrievers. It also included a little Shih Tzu named Spiky, who was the smallest, oldest and the Boss of the Bunch! I had two goldens myself, so I was instantly drawn to them. I was going through a divorce when I found Prada's Bunch on Facebook. I still do not know how I found them, but it was a blessing in disguise.

I have followed them since the very beginning when the puppies had not even opened their little eyes. I watched the puppies grow with their assorted color ribbons on their necks so that Silvia could tell them apart. I saw them having their first solid foods, I watched them climb on toys in the house and go outside for the first time in the grass.

As the dogs got older, Silvia would post pictures of them in her beautiful garden on the patio. She posted videos of the goldens rolling in the grass or taking them on walks with their wiggle butts! All the posts made me smile and brought me comfort. I would talk about Silvia and the Bunch so much to my family and friends that they thought I was nuts because I did not know them personally. I knew them only online!!!

Silvia and I would start private messaging and our friendship grew. Silvia posted pictures of the dogs dressed up in costumes for the holidays, such as Christmas, Valentine's Day, St. Patrick's Day, and Easter. She even had to buy a piece of furniture for her house to keep all the costumes! She would also dress them up in birthday hats and personally wish Facebook followers and friends Happy Birthday with a handmade sign. The videos of the goldens jumping in the pool without permission were favorites of mine. They would not get out of the pool when Silvia told them they must. I loved hearing Silvia's accent telling the Bunch that they were "in big trouble!" They loved to swim and play fetch with rubber shoes and other toys. The videos of the dogs in the green patio chairs for "punishment" were so cute. They would not move until Silvia said they could get down off the chairs.

Our Journey of Love and Adventure

The videos of their birthday parties on January 1 with their party hats and cakes were precious. Silvia has done such a wonderful job training Prada, Charlie and Lalique to become therapy dogs. They help others at libraries, schools, hospitals, nursing homes and so many more places in the Miami area. I look forward to seeing all the pictures on Sunday nights when Silvia has time to post after the weekend adventures.

Silvia is so generous with her time helping people of all ages. Silvia recently created Charlie's Wags of Wisdom and I cannot wait to see its success! I was lucky enough to go with Silvia and Charlie this past Spring to the Honda Classic Golf Tournament in Palm Beach Gardens to work in the Jack Nicklaus Children's Hospital tent. Charlie and Silvia were both rock stars with former patients and other children who visited the tent. Charlie was so sweet letting everyone pet him. He moves his eyebrows in such an adorable way! Silvia and Charlie brought such joy to them as the Bunch did for me years ago and to this day. I was lucky enough to meet Silvia, her husband, Miguel and her son, Carlos. They welcomed me into their home, and we met for lunch as well when I came to Florida to visit family. Though we live far away from each other, we have truly become special friends over the years because Prada's Bunch has brought us together.

We both truly feel blessed to have found each other through social media. Best of luck to Silvia and all her endeavors in the future.

Amy Olswang
Chicago, Illinois

Prada always spread light and love to everyone she knew and to those that knew her via her Facebook page. In this world where negativity can feel overwhelming, just a photo and a caption of Prada and her Bunch was enough to brighten my day and reset my mind. Then the world immediately seemed more loving and kinder. Her Bunch continues her beautiful legacy.

Tiziana Gavin
Adelaide, Australia

Thanks to Facebook and my own love of golden retrievers, I discovered and started following Prada's Bunch and Friends on New Year's Day many years ago. That day Prada had given birth to the most beautiful litter of golden puppies, and I immediately fell in love with Prada, her babies and Uncle Spiky too! Watching Silvia and her beautiful mother bottle feed the baby puppies was so heartwarming — all under the watchful eye of Mami Prada of course. For many years since, I have looked forward to the daily updates and shenanigans that Mami Prada and the Bunch would get into. The photos and videos watching the puppies grow up were often the highlight of my day. Especially when they would insist on jumping in the swimming pool in the morning and make Silvia late for work! Who knew that I could feel such a loving connection to someone else's golden retriever family that I had never even met in person? Prada, her bunch and Uncle Spiky have brought so much happiness and joyful memories into my life and others around the world. When I think of Prada, I cannot help but smile as she was truly one of a kind. I simply cannot wait to read and re-live some of Prada's most memorable moments through the book, Walking with Prada.

Lynne Weber
Pittsburgh, Pennsylvania

These testimonials are based on each person's experience with Prada's Bunch and Friends Facebook page and real-life encounters.

Dedication

"Before you get a dog, you can't quite imagine what living with one might be like; afterward, you can't imagine living any other way."
Caroline Knapp

In memory of my golden retriever, Prada. You made me a better human. My heart soared next to yours during your lifetime. Your love was unconditional and remarkable. I will love you forever, Mami Prada.

To my extraordinary family... My husband, Miguel; my beautiful kids Cristina and Carlos, my furry kids Charlie Brown, Lalique and Oliver; my feathery kids Nina and Cuchi.... You are the steady love in my heart, the unwavering support in my crazy adventures. You loved Prada as much as I loved her. This is our gift to her. You are as much a part of this journey as we were.

To my dear family.... My mom, dad, my siblings.... I am blessed to have you all in my life. You were part of this beautiful journey from the start. Your support was priceless and so appreciated. Mami, Gracias.

To my dear and amazing friends from our Facebook page, Prada's Bunch and Friends... Since the day I posted Prada was having puppies, you were there with me. Your words, encouragement, support, generosity, and love are beyond incredible. Our friendship grew with the puppies. Many years later you are still latent and present to love and support all our adventures. Prada was so dear to all of you. It was my immense pleasure to share her, her kids, and my family with you. I will forever have you in my grateful heart for all your love and support.

Contents

Testimonials	iii
Dedication	xi
Prologue	1
Chapter 1: Growing up Loving Animals	7
Chapter 2: Welcome Home	15
Chapter 3: A Golden Puppy Named Prada and Her Best Friend Spiky	23
Chapter 4: Prada and Me	31
Chapter 5: Prada Becomes a Mom	41
Chapter 6: Prada's Bunch and Friends	55
Chapter 7: Prada and the Unthinkable	73
Chapter 8: Prada's Bunch and Friends' Support Came with Faith, Hope, and Love	85
Chapter 9: Veni, Vidi, Vici - I Came, I Saw, I Conquered	99
Chapter 10: On our Way to make a Difference	111
Chapter 11: Love is a Four-Legged Word	123
Chapter 12: All For the Love of Dogs... and Humans	135

Chapter 13: A loving Paw for the Children	145
Chapter 14: Our journey continues with meaningful stops along the way	157
Chapter 15: Mami Prada and her Magnificent Self	169
Chapter 16: And with Lalique We Are a Team of Four	189
Chapter 17: Our Life Will Not be the Same	209
Chapter 18: Labor of Love by Prada's Bunch	231
Epilogue	245
Acknowledgements	249
Further Testimonials	253
About The Author	261
Speaker Bio	263

Prologue

"Dogs are not our whole life, but they make our lives whole."
Roger Caras

Mami Prada. Her smile, her wagging tail and that beautiful spirit came today to the West Kendall Baptist Hospital full force♡ not to mention the beautiful red pompom on her head♡ nurses love her so much! They even know her favorite spot to scratch!!! She was delighted! 😊

We visited many rooms and received so many nice comments and thanks. Even blessings for what we do.

One lady realized Prada was a survivor after seeing her pink breast cancer patch on her vest and when I told her of Prada's journey, she looked at Prada and said to her, "Ohhh the Lord sent you a guardian Angel, Prada. Your very own mom." ♡

That comment made me smile and I got teary eyes because it is like that. As she is an angel to so many people, I am to her. The lady promised to pray for Prada and blessed us for our work. In every visit, God placed on our way the people who need us the most.

We went to visit another room. There were a few visitors surrounding an elderly gentleman. Prada got in and after looking around went directly to the daughter, who was clearly sad and sat on the sofa next to her. She faced her and gave her paw. The lady was incredibly happy to receive love from Mami Prada. ♡

I really enjoy spending time with people who appreciate our visits and Mami Prada's unconditional love. After almost two hours visiting patients and nurses, it was time to go home.

Come walk with us. You will adore every step of the journey.

Loving dogs is easy. They give you attention, adoring looks, and they make the best and most cuddly friends. But when you look into their eyes and experience that special connection, you feel a tingling in your heart that tells you they know they can count on you, they appreciate it, and they trust you even more.

Our Journey of Love and Adventure

During my time with Prada, I learned a lot about how a dog loves. We found ways to connect that took our relationship to new levels. Then it happened between me and her offspring Charlie Brown and Lalique. We found this special bond that takes an ordinary dog-owner relationship to an extraordinary one.

Since the day Prada came into my life, I knew I had found my soul dog.

Prada was truly special and unique. A golden retriever with soft fur, gentle paws, soulful eyes. She has won my heart since the day she was born and took a piece of it when she passed away. What we experienced together was one of the most special experiences in my life. The amazing journey from her birth, her relationship with Spiky, her dog brother, her kids, and her human family was remarkable. Our life was exuberant with her in it.

We experienced cancer scares and all kinds of remarkable moments. Saying goodbye to her on the day she peacefully passed away was one of the most difficult moments I have ever experienced.

We have touched many lives in many special ways. First, through our journey with our Facebook page, Prada's Bunch and Friends, then, when we found a way to pay back the kindness and blessings we received through the most difficult moments we experienced. We embraced them all.

The best part of our journey was finding our purpose and truly defining mine. Prada and her kids became therapy dogs. We worked extremely hard through training, learning about how the bond between humans and dogs help with healing, and together the four of us found ways to help many people by sharing furry love and compassion.

You will learn a lot about me. About my life, my love for animals and how I came to be who I am today. My strengths and my weaknesses. You will understand why I believe in faith and how sharing my life with so many people gave me the stepping stone into this marvelous opportunity to show what I love. It was and still is so special. My heart is content and fulfilled with peace and love.

You will learn about my devotion to my dogs and how they taught me to be humble and genuine.

After Prada was gone, my relationship with Charlie Brown became stronger. We complement each other, he knows me, and he would absolutely be considered my most precious soul dog, after Prada. Together we have found new meanings through our work as a therapy dog team. We have come across many situations and helped many people, especially children. We became partners in a new journey. Charlie has this peaceful, gentle soul and a set of kind eyes that captivate everyone he meets.

Lalique, my sweet and rebellious girl, took her love for humans to an incredibly special place. The day she visited the nursing home I knew that it was her niche. She adores the elderly friends she visits. She knows them and loves them dearly. They are her people. I love to see how her presence brings light into their eyes.

I have learned so much from all of them. We have shared so many amazing adventures throughout our journey together and with Prada and Spiky. I cannot wait for you to love them the way I do and experience all they have lived through.

To this day, our journey continues full of love and adventures.

Come along, I welcome you into our lives with open arms and a humble heart.

Are you ready? It is time to come *Walking with Prada*.

Our Journey of Love and Adventure

Chapter 1

*"One way to get the most out of life,
is to look upon it as an adventure."*
William Feather

Growing Up Loving Animals

After having five children, you would think my parents' hands were too full to even consider adding a dog or a cat or even a monkey to the mix. But they sure did. I grew up in Barquisimeto, Venezuela. We had a beautiful home full of love, animals, friends, and shenanigans.

My love for animals started when I was a little girl. I used to visit my grandfather's restaurant and run towards the backyard to look for little frogs. I used to be a little naughty; I will confess. I used to grab them and show them to other kids at the playground, shoving them right in their faces. My grandfather was not happy, I was scaring the customer's kids. It was funny, at least to me.

I traveled all over the country with my family on vacations or going with our dad on work trips. We loved those trips! The mountains, rivers, the beach. During the trips we always found ourselves looking for animals. We loved to visit small towns and stay in mom-and-pop hotels. We loved meeting the people who ran them. We loved their cats, dogs, cows, chickens, you name it.

One time we stopped by a road to save a chicken with her little chicks. My little sister even had a conversation with the chicken. It was such a beautiful experience.

We rescued turtles crossing roads and met beautiful horses at the "Fincas," or farms. Our adventures always involved animals. They attracted us like bees to a honeypot.

We used to belong to a horse ranch in the outskirts of our city. It was called Rancho 5A. We had a few horses. Horses are beautiful creatures that are intelligent, strong, and gentle. We were smitten with ours.

We had a spectacular horse named Azabache. He was a huge black horse with a white diamond on his forehead and white socks on his front legs. He was my mom's pride and joy. She loved that horse so much. I learned to ride with him and grew to understand so much about his powerful and gentle heart. Sometimes I would ride him bareback! What an amazing experience. I will never forget those days. We looked forward to the weekends when we got to spend all day riding the horses with friends by the mountains and taking care of the horses. We even took part in horse racing competitions. Friends and family gathered there all because of the love we shared for the horses. It was a family affair.

My sister had one called Ventarrón. He was a force to reckon with. Strong willed but gentle when he wanted to be. It is such a special experience to ride horses and to know you can trust them and count on them to take you places and discover amazing experiences while riding them. We even had a donkey. He was stubborn to say the least, and funny too.

Barquisimeto, my city, has many little towns nearby with pieces of land people cultivate with crops and farm animals. My parents had a piece of land called Mi Tierrita (my little land). We had chickens, horses, a few crops, and a beautiful cow named Mariposa (Butterfly) that loved to give kisses with her very rough and long tongue. You would have to be careful around her or she would take down the buttons of your shirt with one lick!

It was a big adventure when we went there to visit. Feeding the chickens, riding the horses, and playing with Mariposa was such a treat. It was a rustic place. We slept in hamacas (hammocks) and ate cheese made from Mariposa's milk. We took showers with chilly water from the hose and played games at night with the light of lanterns. Unforgettable times living life with my family and loving the land and its creatures. Going there was such a heartfelt experience. Hard work and heartbreak too when an animal got sick or died. It is always so humble to learn from the land and the animals.

Seventeen animals. Yes, that is how many we had at one point in my house. We had dogs, cats, birds, hamsters, a snake — which was my little sister's favorite animal — a monkey and a Scarlett Macaw parrot called Beethoven. It was a small zoo among humans.

Oh, I loved that parrot with all my heart. My dad had a home appliances business and he used to travel visiting his clients all over Venezuela. One day he saw this little bird on the side of the road while he was driving back home. He rescued him and brought him home. I claimed him as mine the minute I saw him! I had no idea if the bird was a boy or a girl, but I decided to call him Beethoven. I was about 14 years old.

It was tiny and had no feathers yet on its body. I fed him milk and bread every day. I kept him in a shoe box by my bed. He grew his feathers and started to talk. He could be very loud. I am sure he made Beethoven and his opera friends proud. He grew up strong and beautiful. Red, yellow, and blue feathers with a beautiful tail and a powerful beak. Needless to say, it was quite an adventure to have him around since he was living in the house just like the dogs and cats. We only put him in his cage when we went out.

Beethoven would follow me everywhere. He went up and down the stairs and flew across the house looking for me when he did not see me right away. When I came home from school, he was waiting for me. We did homework together, which was a challenge since he loved to eat and break my pencils.

I used to bathe him in my shower, dry him with a blow dryer and put baby oil on his feathers. He slept on my bed headboard. In the morning he would wake me up by touching my hair with his beak and saying "Hola" hello. My dad used to come into my room to tell me it was time to go to school. Beethoven was so protective of me that he would walk on my back and opened his wings as if to say, "step back, she is mine." My dad respected him and used to say, "I know, tell her it is time for school."

We were best friends and experienced life growing up together. One day he flew out of the house when I was at school. My mom was beside herself! She spent the entire day on the sidewalk calling him and watching where he was. When I got home, he saw me and flew right down to me. I will never forget how hard it was for me to leave him behind when I had to move to another country. I was so grateful that he stayed with a great family friend and lived an exceptionally long and beautiful life.

When I was about 16, my mom gave me and my sister two small dogs. Mine was a boy named Lee Ying and my sister had Osawa, the girl. Lee Ying and Osawa were purebred Pekinese dogs. Two cute little fur balls.

That breed was fancy and so elegant! Lee Ying was so handsome with his soft gray and white hair and short snout. Osawa was brownish. Lee Ying and I went everywhere together, another special friend that filled my heart with love. I found out about a dog show in town, and I could not wait to show him off! I was so proud of him that I took him to the exhibition. We even won prizes! It sure was an experience!

When we went to college in Caracas, another city far from home, we took Lee Ying and Osawa with us. They were our link to our home and to our family. Coming home to them was coming home for sure. I remember Lee Ying by the door waiting for me when I came to the apartment. It was like he knew I was coming.

When Venezuela took a turn for the worse, my parents, who escaped the Cuban regime when they were young, decided to move all of us to Miami, Florida, to start a new life where freedom is loved and cherished.

My sisters and I went to live with my dad's family in Puerto Rico to study for a year. It was an incredibly stressful time in our lives. All that was familiar was left behind. Our parents sold our home and moved our life away to Miami, where we have lived now for about 34 years. All the animals went to loving homes with friends and family. I was thankful that Lee Ying and Osawa came with us.

When we were finally reunited in Miami with our parents, brothers, and dogs, life got somewhat back to normal. Despite being in quite a different country, I had my family and my dog back. All was well.

We learned to live a new routine, a new language, which was a challenge on its own. Many nights I cried thinking my life was over because I did not understand what people were saying to me. I was not fluent in English, and I had to start over. It took lots of sacrifice and dedication. It was a big relief to have Lee Ying with me, he was my rock. He slept in my bed warming my side and licking my tears. No one would know about my struggles and insecurities. But he did. His little body next to me was all I needed to keep going.

One evening we were looking for Osawa. She was nowhere to be found in the house. When we went outside, we found her in the pool. What a horrible moment. She loved to lay down on the side of the pool and she fell and could not get out. We were all devastated. Lee Ying was so sad. Those were very tough moments for our family. He was then spoiled and loved even more.

While I was still adjusting to my new life, I met Miguel, my husband. He used to come by the house to visit and share fun times with my family. Needless to say, Lee Ying was not too fond of him. It was a challenge to balance the love of my two boys. Lee Ying made sure he sat between us on the sofa and acted like the best chaperone ever. My dad was proud of him. He took that responsibility seriously.

As dogs typically do, digging was something he loved to do. One day Lee Ying went outside to potty, and I got distracted. He decided to dig under the fence and escaped the yard. I was beside myself. I looked all over the area around the house. Driving around the neighborhood for hours. I asked the neighbors and stopped the cars. No one saw him. I had an accounting final that day and all I could think of was Lee Ying. He was lost. And I never found him again. My heart was so shattered I even failed that class. Coming home and not seeing him was a dagger to my heart. I blamed myself for not being careful. I was devastated and hopeless.

I did not get another dog after that. The heartbreak was too deep. Too intense. I never knew how much I could love a dog until the day we parted ways, especially a dog that was there for so many altering moments in my life. First leaving behind Beethoven and then losing Lee Ying made me afraid of that pain. I decided not to have dogs anymore. I was not going to suffer another heartbreak. I thought that I was better that way. Life was hard enough without the animals I grew up with.

A few months later, my mom, who loved cats, got two Persian cats that were so beautiful. One ebony colored called Osito and one butterscotch called Garfield. They were now our furry kids. But cats are cats and these two were highly pompous cats. I loved them but they were not my dog. My faithful companion and friend.

A couple of years passed by. Miguel and I got married

and our daughter Cristina was born while I was finishing college. It was such a busy time in my life. Taking care of a home, a husband, while working during the day and going to school at night. I knew that I needed to keep it together and be strong. My little baby girl needed me so much. When she was one year old, I graduated. I was so proud in my graduation cap and gown with my husband and carrying my girl in my arms. I did it! I carried out something that I thought was impossible.

Our life kept us busy. Carlos was born two years later. We had two beautiful kids that filled our life with so much joy. I had a full plate. I never really thought about having a dog in our lives. We enjoyed our time as a family, teaching them about love, growing up with them, and watching them marvel at life.

Little did I know that God had another adventure with a dog on its way.

Chapter 2

"For me a house becomes a home when you add one set of four legs, a happy tail, and that indescribable measure of love that we call a dog."
Roger Caras

Welcome Home

Our little family grew. The children were growing, and we were still busy. My kids were okay around animals but cautious, especially Cristina. When she was a toddler my sister's dog, a little cocker spaniel, ran towards her and knocked her down. She was very apprehensive of dogs after that.

For me, that was devastating. I never thought that could happen. Dogs are good for people. Being afraid of them was not necessary. That episode made her feel afraid. I was sad that I could not change that. We tried to get her to meet other dogs when we visited family and friends, but she was reluctant. At the end, only she could overcome that fear. I tried to show her how good dogs were, how much love she could get while enjoying playing with a dog, despite feeling skeptical.

One time I thought by bringing a dog home we could work on that fear. We got a golden retriever puppy named Sara. Sara was wild. I could not remember what having a puppy felt like. I had no knowledge on how to care for one. My husband Miguel did not grow up with animals, so we were both at a loss. Sara wanted to play so much. She ran after Cristina. Cristina ran away from Sara. Mayhem! Cristina would be climbing the sofa and screaming, and Sara thought it was the perfect game. Against my better judgement and with a heavy heart I had to choose between my sanity, Cristina's wellbeing, or Sara. So, I decided to call the breeder and return Sara to her original home and pray she found a home with a not scared child in it. It was an extremely hard experience, but I had no choice. I did not have the heart to see my child scream in terror because a puppy was chasing her. I thought we would give her more time. When she was ready then we could try again.

A couple of years passed by and one day I was at the nail salon with Cristina. This place was next to a puppy shop. We passed by and she saw a tiny little dog inside. She stopped for a second and looked at me. She said, "I guess we can go in and meet him." Oh My Gosh!!! This is it! My heart did a flip flop and in we went! We sat on the floor with this little, tiny ball of fur. It was a girl. She was a Shih Tzu. The owner said she was going to be small. That was a reassuring comment for Cristina. White with little black strikes on her body, she was adorable! Cristina was hesitant but she said "Mami. I like her. Can we bring her home? I promise I will not scream." You bet little girl! I did not hesitate. We got her and then we went home. Miguel was confused but happy that Cristina took the step all by herself. We have a dog! She named her Miracle. Her reasoning was that it was indeed a Miracle that she agreed to have a dog at home. Such a blessing! Cristina was always looking after Miracle and things were going great.

Three weeks passed by. Miracle was acting a little weird and got a bit lethargic. We called the puppy shop, and they told us to take her to the veterinarian. The vet said she had parvo; a sickness puppies get. I did not know that at the time, but it is common in puppies bought at puppy stores. I learned my lesson after that.

She got so sick that there was no way to save her and with a heavy heart we had to say goodbye to Miracle. Our hearts were broken. Cristina wrote a letter to God after that. She said "God please take care of my little puppy. I know she would love to be with you." I felt her sadness deeply in my soul.

To be honest, I was in shock. How did this happen? Why did God allow Miracle to die when he knew this was Cristina's miracle? That she finally overcame her fear? I was heartbroken, mad, and hurt on behalf of my little girl. But God had another plan.

We went to the puppy shop looking for an answer. They sold us a sick puppy! The lady was very apologetic and said, "please take this puppy, he is a boy but same size and age as the one you had. I have already checked him with the vet, and he is clear. No worries." He was a gray, white and black faced Shih Tzu with an incredibly special look on his eyes. I was moved by it, so I agreed to take him.

We brought this little fur ball home. Carlos, my son, said that he wanted to name him. We all agreed. He said "Spiky!" Since Carlos was wearing his hair in spikes, he was six and extraordinarily strong willed, he wanted the dog to be just like him.

Welcome home Spiky!

And that is how our journey of love and adventure started with Spiky.

Spiky became such a blessing to our family. We learned more about how to keep puppies entertained, we even had a little crate for him, which he was not fond of. We wanted him to be safe, so we insisted. He needed to learn to stay there at night. Well, easier said than done.

A few months later we got a hurricane warning and we needed to get ready. It was coming strong that night. We gathered the kids and Spiky and bundled up to sleep in our bed for the night. After that, Spiky never went back to his crate. He found his favorite place to sleep. Me, being the softy that I am, of course did not object much. I did like his little furry kisses before falling asleep.

He took turns sleeping with the kids, but in the end my bed was his heaven. We had a new routine. Every night when we went to say good night, we'd read a book, cuddle with the kids, and stay with them for a bit. Then, when all was quiet, we went to sleep.

Spiky grew up to be a very stubborn doggie. He decided when he wanted to go out for a walk and was very vocal about it. He would not stop until he got what he wanted. And of course, I catered to all his demands. He became my shadow and best friend.

It was so much fun to have a dog at home. Cuddles on the sofa, listening to him snore and going out with him were such wonderful times. He loved car rides and loved the wind in his face. And he would let you know exactly where he was supposed to be while enjoying the car rides. On Miguel's lap. He absolutely loved being squeezed between Miguel and the wheel. He was at peace there, watching the outside go by.

We had a cabin in Bakersville, North Carolina. We built it with so much love and traveled there whenever we could. Every time we went, we drove 14 hours. We gathered the kids and Spiky and drove to our mountain.

When we finally made it to the top of the mountain, Spiky was the first to get down. He was finally free! His little legs ran as fast as he could doing zoomies all around the cabin! He was home and so were we.

We decided to call him the King of the Mountain. He loved that place so much. It was so special to see his little tongue hanging sideways after the runs. He was genuinely happy.

Every year we went on vacation to the mountains, and he knew. When he saw me packing, he would run and bark full of excitement.

Cristina was finally growing up and accepting having dogs in her life. She was wonderfully comfortable with Spiky and little by little opened herself to meet bigger dogs. This was a real gift to my heart. It made me feel so happy and blessed that she grew out of her fear. Could we consider another dog? Who knows.

We became so busy with life. Kids were bigger and busier with so many activities after school: dance, baseball, you name it. Work, keeping the house and taking care of the kids, was a double full-time job. One day I was coming home, and I saw a grooming van on one of my neighbors' driveways. It looked so nice and professional. I wrote down the number and decided to call them and see if our Spiky could have a nice spa day. We usually bathed him, and he got his nails trimmed when we visited the vet. But this was...wow! Top of the line spa treatment.

When I spoke to the owner of the van, I was surprised to learn that he was my neighbor. Wonderful, I thought! I got to have Spiky groomed by someone nice. He came home and we started talking. He said he too had dogs and that this was his passion. Taking care of them and helping people take care of their dogs, too. Andres was truly the best groomer ever and came home every month to give Spiky a haircut and love. Spiky looked like a million bucks every time! Spiky knew him so well. It was funny to see him hide when he realized it was Andres at the door. Spiky was not fond of baths.

I was coming home one night, and I saw Andres outside with his dogs. I could not believe my eyes! He had a golden retriever and a collie!!! Oh, they were spectacular. I stopped to chat and meet his dogs. I was in love right then and there. He had a golden girl named Chanel. Yes, a very fancy girl, and a beautiful collie named Gucci. We talked and talked, and I was absolutely fascinated by Chanel. I thought about Sara and got a little sad, since we did not have a chance to see her grow up. Chanel had the gentlest eyes and soul. She was so sweet and very friendly. He said that he wanted to have Chanel's puppies and that soon she would meet her boyfriend. Of course, I said, count on me!!! I will help you take care of the puppies!

I found myself looking for Chanel every time I drove by Andres's house. I even offered babysitting! Chanel came home a couple of times. Cristina and Carlos were so happy to meet her and play with her. I was so relieved! Because you know what was coming next…. I wanted one of Chanel's puppies!

On May 2, 2010, I received a call from Andres. It was time. Chanel was having puppies! Oh, Dear! I remember I was at a school event with the kids and was desperate to go home. I wanted to see Chanel and her beautiful puppies. Thankfully, she did amazingly. She had 13 puppies! As soon as I got home, I stopped by Andres's house, and we saw them. The kids were in awe. They have never seen dogs so little in their life. They were so cute and so fragile. We were totally in love. I took advantage of this magnificent moment to mention that I thought it would be amazing to have one of Chanel's puppies as a companion to Spiky. I held my breath! They both looked at me and said at the same time "For real?" I nodded and said YES! We are going to have a golden

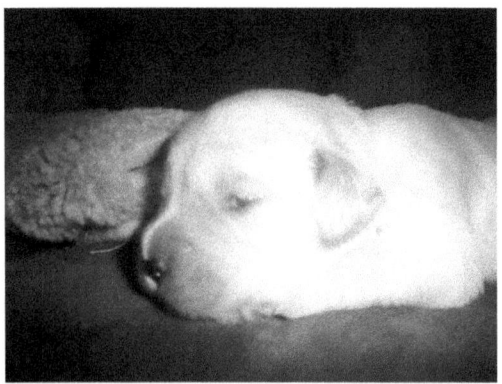

retriever puppy! And not just any puppy. A beautiful gentle golden girl puppy that would grow to be just like her mom.

Every day I visited Chanel and her puppies. I helped Andres feed them goat milk since there were so many of them that Chanel was not able to provide all the milk they needed. We cleaned them and took care of Chanel too. She needed a break from the puppies from time to time. Every week represented a new miracle. More movement, eyes started to open, then eating by themselves, playing with each other. Then the moment to choose our girl came. I had my eye on one that was a light golden color with a beautiful face and super calm. Miguel, the kids, and I went by, and we "chose" her. We debated about what to name her. At the end, we decided she needed to be as fancy and elegant as her mom, so we called her PRADA. That day marked the beginning of a beautiful, amazing life for us.

That is how our journey of love and adventure started with Prada.

Prada was coming home.

Chapter 3

"It is amazing how much love and laughter they bring into our lives and even how much closer we become with each other because of them."
John Grogan

A Golden Puppy Named Prada and Her Best Friend Spiky

Needless to say, you discover pretty quickly that having an older dog and a highly active puppy at the same time is not precisely how you thought it would be.

Prada came home and rocked Spiky's world. He was a grumpy dog. He was okay when you left him alone and did not bother him much. He was already five years old. A mature little dude. Prada pulled his ears, his tail, ate his food and simply did not leave him alone. He even tried to hide under the bed! I did my best to protect him, but it was so dear to see Prada being a happy little puppy going after the old cute grumpy doggie.

This time we were ready for a golden. I was not going to have the same experience that we had with little Sara. This time I knew what to do and how to help her adapt to our home. Thankfully, Cristina was 13-years-old and much better when dogs were around. She saw Prada the day she was born and knew Prada was going to be a good loving doggie. And one of the best sisters ever.

Having a golden puppy is a huge commitment. They are continually active and if they do not get enough training and direction, they can be a bit destructive too. We had to make sure cables, shoes and other important items were out of reach.

We bought Prada a pink collar and leash, bows to put on her little ears and a pink bed. Prada ate the bed, ate the bows, and ate the leash. But we insisted and got her another set. Prada was a force to reckon with.

Anything and everything were in danger from her puppy teeth, yet we loved her so much. It was such a special experience. Her sweet face, fluffy ears and her happiness was so dear to us that any wrongdoing on her part was absolutely forgiven.

She slept in the downstairs bathroom. We added a baby fence to the entrance of the bathroom and that was her room. We did not like the experience we had with puppy Spiky and his crate, so this was a better alternative. This was good for Spiky too. It gave him a break from Prada, the menace girl.

A few weeks later Prada somehow won Spiky's acceptance. She very wisely sat next to him, very calm, as if saying "See Spiky, I am a good girl." So that was the start of their journey. Even though they had their moments, they played, slept together, and would simply lay down next to each other right next to me.

I knew Prada was going to be a big dog, and I knew big dogs needed to learn how to behave better than little dogs. Spiky was Spiky and he was no trouble so I did not think that he needed training at all. I would simply scoop him up and off we went. On the contrary, Prada was going to be big and therefore was ready for training. After researching what to do, I found an affordable option at a local pet store. They had obedience classes for puppies! Excellent! Now we are going to have a perfect and amazing well-behaved golden puppy! Or so we thought.

Prada was a model student. She did puppy classes with much attention. She understood the commands and did everything that was taught. We had so much fun during the classes. She was growing and learning. However, her puppy heart was still very mischievous. At home she loved to find ways to make Spiky run for his life. She loved to eat everything she found on her way. Then she would act innocent and give you puppy eyes, of course. All was forgiven and forgotten.

The first trip Prada took to the mountain was so special. She loved the car ride, sitting with the kids in the back and eating all the snacks she was able to get her beautiful little snout in. We were grateful that she loved to sleep too, which gave some peace and quiet to the kids. Spiky was safe on his favorite spot. Miguel's lap.

As soon as we arrived Spiky showed Prada the ropes. He ran around the cabin and Prada right behind him. Almost like a cat chasing a mouse, it was so special to see them bond in that way. Running through mud and dry leaves, they came back home dirty but so happy.

We did not have a place to keep Prada safe in the cabin living room, so we took her to our bedroom. And then she too found her special place to sleep. In our bed. It was getting crowded for sure. But so full of love. Some nights she would go with one of the kids, however, despite their snuggles, she always came back to us to sleep.

Every day was a fun-filled adventure with her. One day she hid behind the toilet. I could not find her! Even when I called her name, she did not move. Thankfully one of the kids found her and we were so relieved. Scared the daylights out of me!

Prada loved the water. We had a small gentle creek near the cabin, and she loved to run up and down the creek and play with the kids and Spiky. When we went on walks, she was just so happy. Spiky and her ran and played, running up and down the road, smelling the flowers and who knows what else, and then she would find a pond and into the water she went! It was always a mission to get her out.

She really was a ray of sunshine. Everyone in the mountain got to know her and loved our precious golden girl. Prada and Spiky were exhausted at night and would sleep cuddling with the kids while watching TV.

In the mornings, Spiky, being the King of the Mountain, used to run up and down the roads in front of the cabin. Exploring new smells and getting in trouble. He taught Prada to do the same. They would run up the road and when his little legs got tired, they would run back down. By then, I had called their names several times, but they both had selective hearing, I tell you. They came back when they wanted to. If they went too far, we went after them in the ATVs, and they would happily jump in. That was a ride they loved. Snuggling together with the wind in their faces. A perfect ending to a great escapade.

Our Journey of Love and Adventure

One afternoon, Spiky decided to jump off the back of the ATV and hurt his leg. We were so worried! He was limping and crying. We were on a mountain in the middle of nowhere at the time. Thankfully, we had a bit of signal, and we were able to locate a 24-hour emergency vet located two hours from the cabin. We gathered the whole crew and off we went to take Spiky to the vet. When we got there, we registered and told them what happened. I was carrying Spiky the whole time. When I placed him on the floor, he was fine! He walked without complaint and did not even limp for a bit. We were speechless. The little scamp faked all the drama! So, $200 later and another two hours drive, we made it back to the cabin. Prada and Spiky cuddled with the kids and went to sleep. At the end, I was thankful it was no major issue. It really scared me to think about poor Spiky in pain. Moments like that confirmed my belief that I would love and protect my animals like my own flesh and blood. That was a promise I made to each of them the day they came home.

Back in Miami, Prada took her new sleeping arrangements to heart. We tried to get her back to sleep in the bathroom, but she would hide under the bed. I did not have the heart to let her cry and again welcomed her and Spiky into our — thankfully — king-size bed.

Prada grew so fast. She was so intelligent and sweet. We had so much excitement together when we went places. There is nothing like seeing a golden retriever at the store or walking around the neighborhood. People just fall in love with them.

As Spiky, she too loved car rides so much. Her favorite spot was by the back seat, window down and face to the wind. It was very sweet to see them both enjoying the car rides together.

Prada grew taller than Spiky. But that was not really an issue. Spiky continued to be the old wise guy in this relationship. She would follow his lead and he would set the boundaries. However, at the end of the day, they loved and cuddled with each other and rested easily.

They were a funny couple full of mischief and love. They played by chasing each other in the back yard and even though Spiky had little legs, he would keep up without a problem. I loved to see them together. Their friendship was sweet and special.

Since Prada's mom Chanel was living close to us, we frequently visited her. Andres kept one of Prada's sisters. Her name was Fendi. Beautiful girl too. When Andres went out of town, he would leave Chanel and Fendi with us. We had a blast! Three beautiful golden girls and Spiky. Spiky disappeared to Carlos's room when they were with us. Too many high-energy girls for his taste. They played, we took them for walks, and we shared vanilla ice cream.

We kept working on Prada's obedience classes. As she finished all levels her instructor was so proud. Little did he know that she forgot all the training when she got home. We tried to practice, but we were always so busy that we forgave her naughtiness.

One of the things Prada loved the most was a tennis ball. She always had one near her no matter where she went. We played fetch all the time and she was tireless! She used to bring the ball and put it in front of me. If I did not play right away, she would look at me with her puppy eyes and seriously beg me to throw the ball.

Prada discovered that the "puppy eyes technique" was a winner! She would do it for everything she wanted. Whether it was to play, have a snack or go outside, she knew that I would give up just by looking at her profoundly serious face with those adorable puppy dog eyes.

Prada was smart. She knew all her commands and would respond when called. However, when the pool was involved that was another story.

Prada loved the pool with passion. She was a water dog through and through. She would spend hours in it if you let her retrieve toys, balls, even humans. One day she discovered that she could jump in the pool from the side and that was her favorite thing to do. She grew bolder with practice and became a skillful diver. She would look at me asking for me to throw her ball or pool toy so she could dive and retrieve. She also would gather all her toys and place them on my feet. Then she would look at me as if she were saying, "Okay Mom, I am ready! Throw it!" And so, I did. There is not a better feeling than watching your dog enjoy an activity!

Spiky, on the contrary, disliked the pool. He would not get anywhere near it. He would remain inside snoring away while Prada played in the pool with us. He tolerated baths and that was the end of it. His grumpy little face was so special when the word water or bath was said. "No sir, not for me," he seemed to say.

Living with Spiky and Prada was a real blessing to all of us in the family. We found connection, laughter, many times they were the rock when one of us was down. The kids grew up loving our dogs and feeling comfortable embracing their love and support.

Prada gave Cristina the way to open her heart to big dogs, to be able to trust them and be okay around them. Carlos learned to be gentle with them and to respect their space. It was a learning process. As for Miguel, he learned the love of dogs and how important it was for me to know he loved them as much as I did.

Among all the craziness and wonderful times, Prada and I became closer. She knew I was her person and that she felt protected and loved when I was near. That special bond that has so many reasons to be. She turned one year old on May 2, 2011, and by dog standards she was no longer a puppy. But my Prada would have a puppy heart forever. Even through the most amazing and heartbreaking times in our lives.

Our journey of love and adventure had only just begun.

Chapter 4

"A dog is the only thing on earth that loves you more than he loves himself."
Josh Billings

Prada and Me

The day Prada was born, I knew that I would have another special dog in my life. I really missed the connection I had with Lee Ying. The closeness and comfort he gave me through difficult and life altering moments in my life. I still remembered him with love and nostalgia. I adored Spiky but he was our family dog. That special connection was still missing.

All those weeks taking care of Prada, her siblings and mom Chanel was the prelude to an amazing life together. I spent a lot of time cuddling this little girl. When she opened her eyes, and she started to see the world, I was there with her. Playing with her and her siblings was such a joy. After eight weeks she was finally ready to come home and be with me forever.

Prada became my shadow. She followed me everywhere. Closing the door of the bathroom was not an option. She had to make sure I was in her line of vision, and therefore Spiky was also part of the bathroom club. While cooking she lay down right in the middle of the kitchen. It was like having a golden speed bump in my house. Nothing came between us. She was always there.

Sometimes we take dogs for granted. We love them and we enjoy their company. But we do not really realize how deep their understanding can be. How intelligent and resourceful they are. I learned that with Prada. She made me see her not just as a dog but as an intelligent creature.

One day I was sitting on the sofa watching a movie and she was playing with a ball by my feet. The ball went under the sofa, and she could not reach it. She tried to get my attention, but I did not really mind her. Well, she figured it out! She got to the back door and scratched it several times. That was what she did when she needed to go potty. I got up to let her out, but she quickly returned to the sofa and went down to look under it and look at me. She did it. She got me to find her ball. How smart was that?

Like that, she showed me several times that she was capable of so many things. She learned to open the window in the car with her paw. She loved the wind on her face and If I forgot to open the window, she would do it herself.

Prada kept growing up. A beautiful golden girl with light golden fur and a purple mark on her tongue. That fur was all over the house and us. These dogs do shed. You must love it, after all — the dog and her shedding. I called it "Fibers of Love." She had the most beautiful silky fur. Her paws were light and gentle. She would never scratch or paw hard. She would do one thing though; she loved to lick. Prada was a licker! She would kiss to no end! She showed her love by licking faces and hands, and anything in her way. She was pure love.

I decided one day that I wanted to be a runner. I started taking Prada and Spiky for longer walks. After a few walks, Spiky decided that was not for him by sitting in the middle of the sidewalk and refusing to walk. Therefore, Prada became my walking partner with a purpose. We set to walk at least three miles a week. She was awesome the first mile, she was ahead and dragging me. The second mile we walked together and the third mile, it was me dragging her. Needleless to say, we compromised and only walked two miles together.

I started to train more, and she was always there watching me. If I did exercise, she would lay down on the yoga mat. If I were stretching on the floor, she would lick my face and make me giggle. It was quite funny to see her antics.

After several walks, 5ks, 10ks, and 13.1ks, I wanted to take the big step. I had a wonderful group of friends from a Facebook running community. We got together virtually, and we created our own special running club. We trained and encouraged each other. One day, we decided that we were ready to run a marathon. We chose Milwaukie, Wisconsin. There was a race happening in October 2014. Since it was the city one of our group members lived in and it was the closest town to most of the participants, we chose that race. I was in Florida, so it did not matter to me, I needed to get on a plane anyhow. I started training during the summer of that year. It was intense training. I woke up at 5:00 am to go running and beat the summer heat. I ran 12, 15, 20 miles during the weekends. Prada was always by the door waiting for me to return. This training took a lot out of me. Physically and mentally. Mind you, I did not have a runner's body or stamina. I ran purely on will and determination. It was a challenge that made me stronger in so many ways.

One time I came home defeated and ready to quit. That long run, 14 miles, took everything I had to give. I remember I lay down on the floor crying and she lay down right beside me. Licking my tears. She knew I was hurting, and her compassion gave me strength and hope. I calmed down and started to think. I was not a quitter.... I came this far.... I can make things better. I looked at her eyes and said "OK Prada. Time to change strategies. I am going to run this marathon by enjoying the journey. I will not focus on time or pace. I will enjoy my surroundings and I will make this a journey to remember." She wagged her tail and licked my face again. We were back in business. She looked at me like saying "you got this, Mom."

After long runs, I used to dip my legs in the pool to refresh my body. Prada would follow me and stand by the edge of the pool looking to me for the command to let her join me in the pool. And that became our ritual. I came home exhausted, hurting all over, but Prada was there. Ready to be part of my recovery. She waited patiently by the door and waited for me to remove my running shoes and socks. As soon as I opened the back door she ran to the pool and jumped! She was ready to make me smile and to help me find my strength one more time.

As I ran the marathon, which was a very humbling experience, I learned a lot more about myself and my strength. By the way, training in a 95-degree weather and running a marathon in the 30's is not exactly the same. I do not regret it, though. I accomplished the unthinkable and I have the big shiny medal to prove it. This stage in my life served me as the foundation of the strength I needed to muster for what was to come.

My whole family was waiting for me and Miguel to return. Prada's welcome was the sweetest! She cried! She wiggled her whole body; her tail was going 100 miles an hour when she saw me. She was all over me with tons of kisses. The best welcome home reception I got. We did it sweet girl. I ran a marathon, and you were there for me.

Loving Prada was easy. She was this gentle soul. Her face was sweet and delicate. Her eyes spoke words she could not say. Every day was a blessing to have her by my side.

Year after year we celebrated Spiky and Prada's birthdays. They were part of the family and were celebrated as well. Birthday hats and cakes with candles. We had a wonderful time! Prada absolutely loved vanilla cake. She would sit on a chair and wait for her piece. Licking, of course, her plate and hoping for more. The kids had a blast and could not wait to tell their friends that their mom had a birthday party for the dogs.

Prada was a favorite of my mom. She adored my mom and mom her. When she saw my mom arrive and heard my mom's voice, she would cry and wiggle and throw herself on the floor for belly rubs. We had an incredibly special bond, the three of us. Mom knew how special Prada was to me and loved her beyond words. She would bring treats and buy her bows and beautiful bandanas. She spoiled her silly! Whatever Prada wanted, Abu gave her. They were both such a blessing in my life.

Our life kept getting busier and busier. The kids were growing and going to school and after school activities. I was always in a hurry driving the kids around and working on projects. But I never missed a chance to receive love from Prada. She also adored Miguel. They usually sat together on the sofa quietly watching TV. She loved dad's scratches.

When it came to me, Prada had this sense. She would know when I was upset. She would sit by my side or find her way to get herself behind my head if I were on the sofa. She loved to do that. She would climb the sofa and lay down on top of the cushions. She would lay her head down on my shoulder and give me a kiss. Then she quietly stayed there waiting for me to calm down. Her warmth was my calm. Her heartbeat became mine. We were one. I found peace in her embrace.

Our vacations at the mountain were the highlight of the year. We went up there to relax, recharge and enjoy our family time and connect with Nature. Enjoying the peace and quiet of the mountain, the fresh air, the sweet smell of the flowers and the song of the birds in the morning. The best part, we had our whole family together. The kids, the dogs and us. It was an unforgettable time full of laughs, mischiefs, and time with each other enjoying dinner together and cuddling on the sofa with the dogs, reading a good book. We used to hike and explore the mountain. Prada and I loved to walk and run together. After a long walk, we used to dip our "paws" in the creek. She was my best sidekick. We came back home refreshed and ready to face the music of life.

I had such a beautiful experience taking care of Prada and her siblings when she was born, that I decided I wanted to have Prada's puppies! She was four years old and ready to be a mom. Andres helped me look for a beautiful golden boy to be Prada's boyfriend.

I took Prada to the vet to make sure all was well. The day she was set to meet her beau, I gave her a bubble bath and we were ready to meet a handsome boy named Fredde.

Fredde was a copper-colored golden retriever with a beautiful coat. He was a sweet dog. We introduced them both and it was love at first sight. You know what I mean… We were sure puppies were coming!

With Andres's help, I learned how to keep Prada healthy through her pregnancy. We gave her the right food, vitamins, and took all necessary steps to make her stronger. She was glowing! She was getting big, but she was still her beautiful self. A happy girl with so much love to give.

Spiky was a little confused. Why was Prada not as active as before? Hmm, something was going on. He had no clue he was about to become Uncle Spiky.

The days passed and she became bigger and bigger. We were all so excited! I started to worry. Was I doing the right thing? Watching YouTube videos of goldens having puppies was a bit intimidating. But I trusted God and my gut, and we got ready.

She was due in the first week of January. We had time to prepare. Andres helped us set up the whelping box. It was beautiful! It had wood-like vinyl panels and a plastic tube around the inside. I learned that that was important in case the little puppies got in behind the mom and prevented her from squeezing the puppies.

I got blankets, pads, ribbons, and all the necessary things that I researched and learned from videos.

Prada was doing great! Just a little difficulty walking with her big belly. We assumed she may be carrying 8-10 puppies. The last vet visit went well, and she was ready. She got so much love from the family during the Christmas holidays. Everyone was so excited! It was the first time we had puppies in our family. My mom was worried about Prada. She called every day and came over to spoil Prada and Spiky with delicious treats. We were looking forward to meeting the puppies soon!

Dogs have a unique way of letting you know they are almost ready to give birth. By December 29, Prada started a process called nesting. She would get inside the whelping box and paw at the blankets like she was trying to dig. Mother Nature is incredibly wise. She was letting me know that we would have puppies soon.

In the morning of December 31, 2014, Prada woke up a little slow and acting weird. She was searching around the yard and digging. I gently directed her to the whelping box, and she would do it again.

I called the vet and told him. He said that was normal and that she may have the puppies in a day or two. And he said, "By the way, I am going to be out tonight. I am not going to be available." That made me a tiny bit nervous. My friend Andres was out of town too. Everyone had plans. It was Prada and me. And Miguel and Spiky, who were great moral support, but not that helpful! Okie dookie, Prada was in charge, and I was her assistant.

I remembered that I followed a golden retriever page on Facebook. I posted that Prada was about to have puppies. So many people commented with encouraging words and tips. I was a nervous wreck, but by the same token, I was ready.

Let's do this Prada! I am here for you! Let's welcome these amazing puppies to the world.

Our journey of love and adventure was about to get more exciting and precious!

Chapter 5

"Happiness is a warm puppy."
Charles M. Shulz

Prada Becomes a Mom

The puppies decided to join the world with a big entrance on New Year's Eve! Welcome 2015... You got puppies!

About 11:45 pm on December 31, 2014, labor started. Prada delivered three puppies a few minutes before midnight and the rest after that. Mother Nature is amazing. Prada knew exactly what to do. I had everything ready in case I needed to help her. But Prada was in charge. My job was to make sure the puppies were breathing well.

After she cleaned them, I placed them by her nipples to drink their first milk. One after another they came. By 4 am I had 10 beautiful puppies!

I was so in love and in so much wonder. What an experience it was to see these fragile little puppies so perfectly coming alive into the world.

Throughout the delivery, I asked questions to my new Facebook friends. Everyone was so nice and helpful. They told me what to do and what to look for. How to help Prada with the placenta and how to position the puppies so they were all equally spread out to drink her milk. I got so much support. I was so grateful that I thought of doing a post on Facebook. It was a lifeline for Prada and me.

I placed colored ribbons on each puppy. I identified them if they were male or female and wrote the information while Prada was basking on them and fiercely licking and cleaning. We got this! She was done. No more puppies were coming out.

Then, six hours later she started contractions again. A stillborn puppy was born. I was in shock, and I was beside myself. Prada was agitated licking it and trying to get him or her to react. But it was dead. I cried helplessly. I did not know what to do to save it. When I was trying to rub him, Prada took it out of my hands. And something that I never knew could happen, happened. She started to eat it. I was in shock! I took it away and she was so frantic. Later, I learned that they do that in the wild. It is an instinct to protect the ones alive from predators, so they do not come near the puppies that are alive because of the smell. She is an animal after all.

After that, another came. Also, dead. My heart really lost it. But I knew nothing could be done. I took it away before she had a chance to see it.

We focused on taking care of the other 10 puppies. I made sure Prada had water, food, and lots of love. Prada did not miss a beat. She was very attentive, licking them and checking each of them and always aware of where they were.

I placed them in warm blankets in a laundry basket while I cleaned her and the whelping box. She never took her eyes off them. We were learning a new routine. She knew I was ok to be near them.

That first day was a very emotional one for my family. The kids were older already and they went out to celebrate New Year's with friends. When they returned, they found puppies at home! What a special moment for all. They were so excited!

Spiky, on the other hand, was not impressed by the commotion and the puppies and decided it was best to keep dad's company by the sofa.

I posted an update again on the golden retriever page on Facebook. Many of the new friends from my first post commented and were so happy to see the puppies well and Prada doing better. Posting became part of the routine too.

Every morning I would clean the whelping box. I placed the puppies in the warm blankets in the basket and Prada sat near them. When I took too long, she would pick them up and bring them one by one to the whelping box. It was so endearing to see her mother's instincts.

A few days later, I noticed that she started to feel weak. It was hard for her to stand sometimes. I decided to take her to the vet. The vet thought it was calcium deficiency and gave her a shot of calcium and something that helped eliminate the placentas she ate. I took her home and was keeping an eye on her. The next day, she got even more lethargic and feverish. I panicked! I knew I would lose her if I did not hurry up.

I took her to an emergency vet. They did a blood test and x-rays. The vet told us that Prada was anemic and had an infection in the uterus. Prada needed to take strong antibiotics therefore she could not nurse. Oh, I was devastated. But at the same time, I was relieved that Prada was going to be okay with this treatment.

Now what do we do?

At that moment, our mission started. We needed to save the puppies no matter what.

I posted on Facebook and got some ideas. I got formula but they would not drink it. We had a truly brief period to figure it out. I remembered we used goat milk for Prada and her siblings, and they liked that very much. I hurried up and got the goat milk and hoped for the best. I learned quickly how to feed them in little bottles and every three hours we had a feeding shift. Miguel, the kids, and I fed them with the bottles. Thankfully, our guardian angel, my dad, became the "Goat Milk Whisper." He would go around town checking all the supermarkets for the same goat milk. He came home one time with 20 cartons! I was so grateful for his help.

The only downside was that Prada needed to be out of the whelping box. That was a big challenge. We figured out a way to keep her outside the whelping box and keep her next to us. We created a system. I placed the puppies in the basket, and she would sit next to them. She calmed down a bit and understood her assignment. We were a team. After we finished with the bottle and burped them, she cleaned them and stimulated them, and I placed them one by one back in the whelping box with blankets and a warmer pad.

It was so hard to keep them apart. She longed to be with the puppies. She did not understand why I had to keep her out. She would look at me with her beautiful eyes asking for permission. I gave her love and cuddles and told her all was okay. Once the feeding was done and the puppies were asleep, she would lay down inside the basket with the warm blankets to be near them.

I had to return to work after the holidays, so thankfully, my mom gave me a hand during the day. My whole family took turns feeding the puppies. My mom cooked for Prada and fed her by hand. She was so distressed that she did not want to eat on her own. The pitiful thing cried wanting to get in the whelping box, always breaking my heart. But that was not possible. They could not drink her milk since she was taking strong antibiotics. I cuddled her on the sofa and placed ice packs to help with inflammation. It was extremely hard to see her suffering.

We had seven girls and three boys. We named them based on their ribbon colors. Miss Pinky, Miss Ruby, Miss Magenta, Miss Goldy, Miss Teal,

Miss Peachy and Miss Lily, were the girls. Mr. Brown, Mr. Blue, and Mr. Green were the boys.

A week later, one of the girls, Miss Pinky, started to get weak. She did not want to eat. I tried everything to no avail. During the night I lost her. It was another devastating moment. I have never cried so much or felt so impossibly sad. My brave little soul. I cannot describe how much my heart ached. I posted on Facebook and many reassured me that it could happen. Some people were harsh and blamed me for not saving her. But many assured me that it was not my fault. I tried everything possible. It was a very emotional and difficult night.

I needed to keep the other puppies alive. We fed them goat milk and cared for them with love and gentle hands. I weighed them to make sure they were eating enough to gain weight which was so important at that stage. A week later Miss Goldie started to show the same signs as Miss Pinky. Not wanting to eat and feeling lethargic.

This time I did not take chances. I found the best veterinary office near me and rushed in with her. I was so worried and desperate. We were blessed to have found the most caring and wonderful doctor and her team. They took blood from Miss Goldie and told me she had anemia and that she may have gotten it from Prada when they were feeding. The only way to save her was a blood transfusion.

I spoke with my family, and we knew that we needed to try anything to save her! I agreed with the vet and the procedure began. Let's do it. Our precious girl received the transfusion, and after a few hours Miss Goldie started to feel better and immediately became more active and hungrier. When I returned home, I noticed Miss Magenta had the same problem. I called the vet and ran with her back to the office. Thankfully, they were waiting for us, and they did the blood transfusion, too. Luckily, one of the vet's assistants had a Great Dane that donated enough blood to keep just in case. (I will always be grateful for that big boy). By now the vet was so concerned! She said, "They could all die if we don't do something"

I said, "Not under my watch. Now, what can we do?"

I came home with vitamins with iron. We gave it to all the puppies to try to avoid a downfall. A few hours later, I realized Mr. Green was already weak. It was already the weekend and thankfully the vet agreed to help us, again. We rushed to the vet on a Saturday night. Mr. Green got a transfusion, too.

We were definitely fighting against all odds. However, we saved them all.

The rest started to feel better with the vitamins, so no more fears. They were going to survive! Thank God.

We kept feeding them every three hours with goat milk. I spent all those weeks sleeping on the sofa so I could feed them on time. Prada started to improve and get better. A great relief. They were growing and soon they were opening their eyes. They were becoming more active and drinking more milk.

Meanwhile Prada was always attentive and wanted to be with them. Much to my regret, she was still on antibiotics and unable to nurse them.

One day I felt so bad that I dressed her in a one-piece bathing suit so she could join her sweet puppies, even though nursing was forbidden. It was so

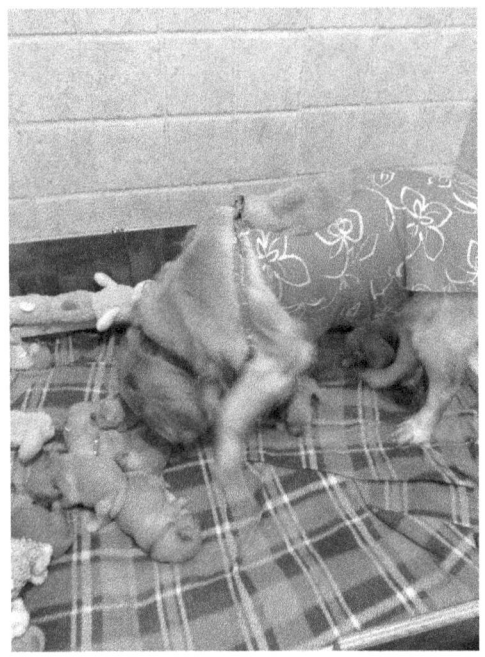

funny seeing her dressed in a red bathing suit prancing around. I allowed her to get in the whelping box, and she had the most amazing time cuddling with them. I did the best I could! And it worked. Prada was content and I was elated.

They were getting hungrier and more demanding. I posted about it, and someone suggested I get a big aluminum plate shaped like a donut. It is a special plate for puppies to drink milk. I ordered one and the next day I filled up the plate with milk and then placed the puppies around it to eat. They wasted no time!

They started to learn how to drink by themselves! And with this new phase, the mess got bigger. They were walking around more and becoming more curious too. They were funny, loud, and happy puppies. I often laughed when I saw them playing and creating mayhem. The poop piles were also bigger, but I did not care. I had a smile from ear to ear, since now I knew they were each eating their share.

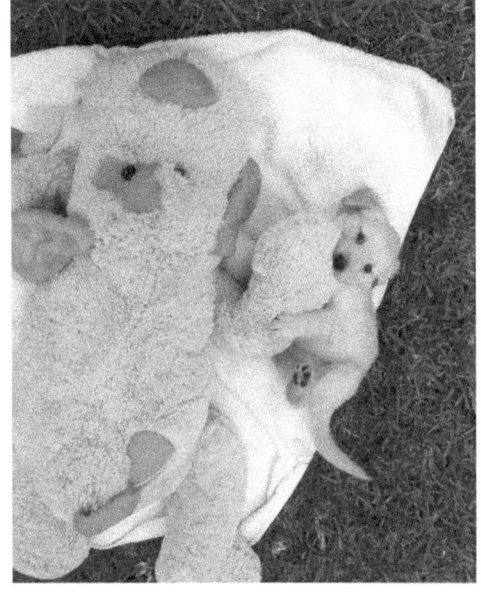

We had a huge play pen in the middle of the living room where all of them had space to play and sleep. They played with each other and even fought with each other. They were rambunctious! It was amazing. I got them this huge stuffed puppy. We called it Mr. Lovey. He became an incredibly special friend to the puppies. They snuggled with it, hid underneath and played with its ears. They absolutely loved it. They had a bunch of toys in their play pen as well and a little slide! Oh, so much fun! I snapped pictures every day and posted them for our new friends.

My whole life was turned around. Everything became secondary. My mom, my dad and my sister, Luly, were a huge help. My mom came over every day, helping me while I was at work, feeding Prada and making sure they got what they needed. My family took turns feeding, too. I remember rushing after work to go to them. It was incredible. Lots of work but lots of smiles while watching their antics. I posted their new adventure with pictures and funny statements. By then I saw many familiar names in the comments. We got followers!

When they were five weeks, Prada was playing with Miss Teal. Unfortunately, she was a bit rough and hurt Miss Teal's head. We rushed to the emergency vet, but it was too late. The damage to the brain was severe. It was impossible for her to survive.

I lost another one. It was a roller coaster of emotions. I knew it was not Prada's fault. We had taken her out of her maternal environment therefore she was not capable of acting like a regular mom. I had separated her from the puppies, and she was not familiar with the game. I thought that was the right thing to do.

Later, I realized it was a huge mistake to keep her apart. But I was so afraid. I did not want to risk another incident. I was not an expert, and everything was new to me. As they say, it was trial and error. Definitely, the loss of her puppies cut me to the bone.

They grew. We started solid foods and things got even busier and messier. Yes, a state of disarray during every feeding.

Everything revolved around them. There were very tough and incredible moments. The puppies were so fragile. No one would think that could be the case, but they were.

We fed, cleaned, and watched every one of them. Making sure they were well.

At night, I had a special routine with them. I would take them one by one, wash them with warm soapy water, dry them, and give them a kiss before placing them back in the pen. After that, they would snuggle with Mr. Lovey and each other until they fell asleep. I used to look at them sleeping and thought to myself, they are truly a miracle. My miracle.

It was time to take them to the vet for checkups and vaccines. It was an adventure to say the least. My mom and I loaded them inside laundry baskets. We placed them in the back seat of my car. You can only imagine the crazy time we had gathering them back into the baskets to take them down to the vet's office. They were these incredible little bundles of joy. The office was in heaven. Doctors and nurses got on the floor with them to receive tons of puppy kisses. They were thriving! Good weight and all healthy. A total blessing and peace of mind for us.

Things got very hectic with the puppies becoming bigger and more active. They ran around in the yard, finding little sticks and stealing flowers from my flower bed. They were little rascals in disguise.

At night, I opened the play pen and let them run into the kitchen and living room. We had this special game with plastic cups. They loved running around with them so much and creating a big mess. They loved to steal my shoes too and chew the shoelaces. Uncle Spiky was in the middle of it all. Keeping a watchful eye but also his distance. Those little rascals were always after his tail and ears. He had flashbacks of Prada when she was a puppy! Prada sat on top of the sofa, watchful and happy.

And just like that, eight weeks came around. It was time to go to their new homes.

I chose every family with care. I defied destiny for them. I needed to make sure they were loved and cared for in the most special homes.

I was going to keep Miss Magenta and Mr. Green. Mr. Brown was going with the puppies' dad's family. Miss Lily was going to live with my friend Lulu who is a photographer. Our deal was that I let her have Miss Lily in exchange for photoshoots for the puppies. It was a perfect deal! Miss. Ruby was going to live with my parents. My mom was so smitten with them that she wanted one of her own. Miss Goldie, Miss Peachy and Mr. Blue were going to live with close friends.

The day that Mr. Brown was going to his home with Fedde's parents I got a call from the dad. They were going to have a baby and the mom was having a rough pregnancy. They decided to sell Mr. Brown to someone. Oh, my heart sank. How could I give away my Mr. Brown to a stranger? That is not what I wanted. I was frantic! This boy was one of my favorites. We had such a deep connection. But God had a plan.

We had a family meeting and decided to buy him from the dad's parents. Mr. Brown became ours. Prayers were answered! Then I had three puppies! It was going to be a bit overwhelming to say the least to have five dogs at home. Miguel was having palpitations thinking about the food and vet bill. I was in love with my puppies! I would have kept them all!

My oldest sister, Maribet, was going to get Miss Teal from the start. But since we lost Miss Teal, sadly she was not going to have a puppy. Everyone else was taken. I convinced my sister to take Mr. Green. This will bring peace to my heart since he would still be with the family. Mr. Green was as lucky as a pot of gold. He was going to have a wonderful mom and two awesome brothers.

Each of them went to their forever homes with a contract that made the new parents responsible for the puppy with a promise to return him or her to me if it did not work out. I made sure everyone knew that I would always look after them. And I did. Even my parents signed the contract. Every month, I checked on the puppies and even to this day, I still do.

Before they left, we had the most amazing and beautiful puppy photoshoot with Spiky and Prada as well.

The puppies got their first grooming bath, courtesy of Andres, a happy and proud grandfather. Then we set up the photo background, got bows on the girls' ears and tiny bandanas for the boys. It was adorable! We placed them in a huge wooden basket! They looked like sweet presents. Everyone was in love. My friend Lulu, Miss Lily's mom, took the most beautiful pictures of them all. I even got one with them. I was beaming! I was as proud as I could be of my little tykes.

Our Facebook friends were excited and in love with their first photoshoot! The post went viral! It was extremely hard to see them go. But I was happy. They each had a good loving home.

I posted about each farewell. Pictures of the new parents and their happy loving embrace carrying each puppy. Tons of people mentioned that they

were sad and even upset that they were not going to know more about the puppies. They were invested in our journey. One person mentioned that he absolutely loved Prada's Bunch. Each puppy won the heart of our Facebook followers.

I loved that name! Prada's Bunch. It was exactly what they were. A beautiful bunch of puppies of my sweet Prada!

After that post, I researched a bit about Facebook and realized I could create a page for the puppies.

On March 2, 2015, after almost nine weeks, our Page went live. Prada's Bunch and Friends was created so all the friends that saw them grow could have news of them. The first day we got 500 followers! And it is still going strong after eight years with more than 4,000 followers!

This journey changed my life. My home and life were total havoc. I learned so much. I cried. I laughed. I felt exhausted, hopeless, and faithful, but at the end so proud. Every time I remember what we went through, I remember each of the puppies' faces and Prada's happy smile and wagging tail. I thank God for this journey.

Our journey of love and adventure continued.... with Prada's Bunch in the most amazing way.

Chapter 6

"Be kind and merciful.

Let no one ever come to you without coming away better and happier. Be the living expression of God's kindness."
Mother Teresa

Prada's Bunch and Friends

I missed my little rascals. Their mischief and their amazing capacity to create a mess. But make no mistake. I still had four of them and they were more than capable of creating havoc on their own.

I thanked my lucky stars that Miss Ruby went to my mom and dad's home. They were thrilled to have this little bundle of joy in their home. Miss Lily went to my friend Lulu's home. Mr. Blue went with a little boy and girl, and their family, and Miss Goldie went with a super cute girl and her family. All were in loving homes with the best families.

I still had with me Mr. Green, Miss Peachy, Miss Magenta and Mr. Brown. They were rambunctious, loud, funny, and so adorable! We had so much fun together. Miss Peachy stayed for another week with us and Mr. Green for a couple of months afterwards. They too were going to be happy as a clam in their new havens.

It was time to give their forever name to the puppies!

We decided that Mr. Brown needed to have somehow the word "Brown" in the name. He was really used to it! He got in so much trouble I called his name no less than 100 times a day. That is when we decided to call him Charlie Brown. Oh! We loved it! He did look like Charlie Brown. Soft, funny, and super cool!

Now, Miss Magenta, our other puppy girl, needed a very elegant name just like her grandma Chanel and her mom Prada. We thought about many of the fashionable names until I remember my sister-in-law Olga gave me an expensive and sophisticated perfume called Lalique. Ta da!!! That would be her name! Later, one of our dear friends of Prada's Bunch, Corine, sent me a picture of a store in Cannes on the French Rivera, with the store name. LALIQUE. She found out that is also a very exclusive crystal in France. Well, mission accomplished! We got her the most beautiful, elegant, and exclusive name.

Mr. Green's name was chosen by his two brothers. They wanted a cool short name that represented a boy with lots of mischief in him. And that is how Mr. Green became Jack. Jack is short and easy to call when he gets in trouble!

Miss Lily was such a cute name that her mom decided to keep it. But she added a second name. A special one. Chanel. Her grandma's name. It really sounds special. Lily Chanel. She was soft, petite and such a love bug!

Miss Ruby. She kept her precious name. My mom named her from the beginning and since her ribbon was red, it was a perfect match. Ruby was such an incredible and gentle puppy. A gem indeed.

Miss Peachy was going to a wonderful home in North Carolina. A family that was friends with Andres, my friend and grandfather of the puppies. They named her Lettie Jo. Later, her mom got sick and could not keep her. We found an amazing new mom that lived in the same state. Lettie Jo became Locket. It was a wonderful match.

Mr. Blue had two super cool kids, so he got a super cool name. His name was Max. He was funny and a legendary bowl thief during his puppy days.

And then it was Miss. Goldie. Her new sister was so sweet and named her Molly. They were inseparable since the first car ride home. Two goldies in a pod.

Ok, then! We had Prada, Spiky, Charlie Brown, Lalique and Jack with us. It was mayhem and amazing! A beautiful bunch of golden kids and Uncle Spiky.

That was when our Prada's Bunch and Friends page on Facebook took off with immense success! Our followers were ready for some puppy love and mischief, and they got plenty.

Every morning we posted our "good morning post" it went something like this:

"Good morning ☼ ♡ they woke up very vocal this morning! And they already know how to scratch the door for attention! 🙈 (They were playing around and closed the bathroom door by themselves 👍) breakfast was done and now they are playing a bit in the yard. They found greener pastures! Meaning the other palm tree 🌴 where they can explore more! They chase each other for toys even though there is another toy lying next to them. Just like kids. 🙀 Uncle Spiky ventures outside. They talked for a bit. But he is in the "don't mess with me kid 😡" stage. I had a conversation with Prada. She went up by herself and who knows what she did 🙈 I think the bathroom trashcan may have something to do with it 🐶 they are growing and becoming stronger. I love my rascals! "

Pictures of all the mischief went with the posts.

Some other posts in between of more pictures and videos of their daily adventures, and then, our good night posts:

"Good night ♡ as always mischief was in order 🙈 they chased each other, pulled each other's tails and ears, and made me chase them all over the yard when it was time to come in! 😆 They even tried to hide from me behind the toilet ♡ I had to turn off the bathroom light like I used to do with the kids so they would settle down and sleep. Tomorrow is a new day for mayhem 👍 have a nice rest! For me it is laundry time 🧺"

These posts were amazing. I loved sharing with the world our adventures. For me it was a way to journal the aftermath of such a surreal time during the eight weeks they were growing.

On March 9, 2015, we celebrated my birthday. To this day, that is still my favorite birthday and my favorite birthday picture. We placed birthday hats on the puppies, and then each of us carried one puppy. We placed Spiky on the table and Prada on a chair. We had a cake with sparkling candles! We all gathered and squished together behind the table and sang happy birthday! It was crazy! I had the puppies, my human and furry kids, my parents, and Miguel. It was priceless! A birthday that I will never forget.

Every day was an adventure. With ups and downs and lots of moments that I would cherish forever.

There was a lot more going on than what I posted. I was worried about Prada. She was not really taking well sharing me with the puppies. Sometimes she would hide upstairs in the room to avoid them. Sometimes she would growl at them if they got too close or sit on a chair to avoid them. Spiky was overwhelmed too but that was really his personality. He was grumpy and loved his quiet time. He never hid from the puppies but never let them bother him either. They were about the same size and a lot bolder and more mischievous. They were learning boundaries with Uncle Spiky.

I was really feeling guilty because at the time when they were growing up, I felt that separating them was the best way to keep them safe. It was a mistake that I paid dearly afterwards.

I brought home a friend of mine who was Prada's trainer at the local store. I was looking for an answer or a quick fix. I asked him to come and help me figure out her behavior. He was clear. Nothing would work until Prada accepted them. Only time will tell.

I used to take a break from it all to spend time alone with Prada. Cuddling with her in bed and giving her treats. Taking her for car rides and walks. I needed to make her understand that she was not replaced. She was still my heart dog. My best friend. My everything.

Little by little things started to settle. The puppies learned their routine and among the mischiefs and laughs we made it work.

Every day was a new adventure. I woke up to those beautiful smiley faces. After breakfast I settled them in the play pen and went to work. I came home during lunch to feed them and take them out to potty and play for a bit. Prada and Spiky watched them from the sofa. I rushed home again at 5:00 pm to be with them. Luckily, I worked really close to home and that was a big blessing. At the end of the day, it was time for dinner and shenanigans.

We got this amazing and super fun picture of the three puppies hanging from the fence that blocked the bathroom door. The three of them were smiling. Our followers called them "The Three Amigos." That picture went viral! Even when I reposted it a few years later, many people said it was still their favorite!

We had the occasional upset tummy. One day I found some sort of soft poop and could not tell who that was from, they went potty all over the yard and I could not keep track of who did what. Things got interesting. I had to watch each of them like a hawk. Thank God I became good friends with our vet Dr. Vazquez. She was a godsend to me. She reassured me that it was nothing to worry about.

Maybe one of them ate something that they were not supposed to. Oh dear! Like babies, anything can affect their tummies. We got medicine for everyone, and in a few days, they were all back to normal.

Puppies being puppies, they loved to find things to bite and chew. Shoes, remote controls, charges, magazines, all were subjects to their merciless puppy teeth. Eventually, the ottoman and the sofa were included in the list. Not to mention their new beds. They were a menace, just like their mother when she was their age.

Prada was still apprehensive, especially of Lalique. I guessed that since she was the other female, Prada was not trusting her. But Lalique did not care. She wanted to play with her, no matter what. It was a bit stressful to keep an eye on that situation. I prayed and hoped Prada would accept her. They were so beautiful together.

The kids were stronger and getting bigger. It was time to introduce them to the pool!

Prada, as you know, was a master pool diver. She loved the pool and showed the kids how to swim. They loved it! And they also loved the mud they created by running wet over the dirt and grass chasing each other.

That is when we started the "you are grounded" ritual. They each would sit on a chair, and I would lecture them on their misbehaviors. I used to post the video of them full of mud in their chairs giving me puppy eyes and finished the post with: "it is time now for the Serenity Prayer." This post was another favorite! Friends of the page defended the kids and gave on their behalf millions of excuses. It was truly so much fun! Of course, I never grounded the puppies. How could I? They were angels!

Pool time was a big favorite for all our friends. We played and then it was time for a bath. They sat on chairs while I cleaned up and set up the bath station. Afterwards, everyone went inside and wrapped up in towels and blankets they settled for a nap.

And just like that, many more posts of so many funny moments, crazy moments, sentimental moments, and extraordinary moments.

Prada became Mami Prada to all our friends. Such a dear name. It meant love and dedication. I was mom and we both shared the most amazing title a woman and a dog could have.

Our Journey of Love and Adventure

We celebrated our Facebook friends' birthdays! I had these foam signs that I made with our birthday friend's name. I hung it on one of the puppies and they all sat at a table and chairs with their birthday hats on. Sometimes, Prada and Spiky also joined the fun. It was so great! People loved those posts so much and would share their birthday wishes with their family and friends. We celebrated so many birthdays! It was such a wonderful thing to receive a message asking for a birthday post. And we gladly obliged.

It was time for our summer vacation at the mountain in North Carolina. This was one of the unforgettable ones! We loaded the car with the human kids, three puppies, Prada and Spiky. I was so grateful that Miguel loved us. It was crowded in that car, to say the least. Thankfully, we had an SUV with plenty of space. We lowered the back seats and made a huge cozy bed for the puppies. Prada was in the second row with the kids and Spiky was in his favorite place, Miguel's lap.

We took 18 hours to make it to the cabin. Lots of potty stops. It was a mission. We took them down one by one. Sometimes they only sniffed but no potty. Getting them back in the car and making sure the others did not escape was tricky business. Not to mention we took breaks for treats and water as well. I will say it again. It was a mission.

We finally made it to the cabin! Spiky, the King of the Mountain, was in charge. He took off and after him followed Prada and the three puppies. Oh boy! The humans were all over the place trying to corral them! After a while, we finally got them inside. At this time, I was ready for a strong drink and a nap!

The next morning, the mountain adventure did not disappoint. Spiky, feeling right at home, ran away. Prada escaped after him. Luckily, the puppies were still in the play pen but not for long. It was time to go potty. So out we went, and they went straight to a string of water that was running down the mountain and crossing our backyard. Well, that became Lalique's favorite spot. Every time she went out, she went there and splashed on the muddy water. At this time, I just gave up and kept a bunch of towels by the door.

Our Journey of Love and Adventure

Prada and Spiky came back and we all had breakfast. We took an extra nap, and then we went walking through the roads of the mountain. This time I made sure to get them all on leashes and we tried our best to control the chaos. When we knew it was safe, we let them run to their heart's content. It was wonderful. Spiky and Prada were vigilant and kept them in line. Making sure they did not wander off into the woods. They went up and down the mountain, smelling and enjoying the crisp morning air. Like with Prada, the pond was a major attraction to them. Prada jumped right in and after her the three puppies. Spiky kept barking at them from the sideline. How precious they were. All splashing and playing. My heart was full.

All these adventures made Prada less guarded and more open to playing with the puppies. That was such a relief since I was always observing her behavior. One night I was sitting in the living room watching them play when I saw something so

special... I held my breath. I could not believe my eyes! Prada was laying down in her corner on her mat and Lalique came very calmly and just sat really close to her. Prada looked at her and lowered her head. Then both fall asleep. I closed my eyes and thanked God.

They used to play chasing each other on the porch and Prada, finally feeling happy and resigned, would join and even Spiky joined in the mayhem! It was chaotic and so much fun! I was happy. Finally, my Prada understood that the puppies were part of the family and that her place was never taken.

We had so much fun on that trip! We had a little truck called a mule. It had two seats and a cargo box. We loaded the puppies and Spiky in the back and Prada with me and Miguel in the front. They got to experience so many new smells and unusual places. Wind in their faces. Finding wood sticks and trying to chase the occasional wild animal that dared to show up.

At night, the kids snuggled with the puppies watching TV, after playing and having so much fun. Miguel and I sat and talked on the porch looking at the beautiful stars and being so grateful for the blessings we had as a family.

Every night, I posted about our daily adventure. The comments were hilarious! Everyone was so happy that they got to come along with us on our vacation. It was like a little window where they could look in and bask with us in our happiness.

It was time to go back home to Miami. We were all sad and reluctantly went in the car. At this time, they knew their places and fell asleep soon after we hit the road. 18 hours later.... We were back home. Back to a familiar place and back to our routine.

I posted we were home safe. Our friends were so happy and relieved. They cared about us in such an amazing and dear way.

A couple of weeks later, it was time for Jack to go home to his family. We were sad. This boy was so sweet and Charlie's best friend. But everything was well. He was going to be loved and cherished and would have so many wonderful memories of his own with his mom and brothers.

In October 2015, we decided to have a family reunion for our first family photoshoot. We invited the siblings that were in Miami and had the most beautiful and special time. I made angel costumes for each of them! Spiky looked extremely cute in his special wings and halo. After many attempts, we managed to place them all in chairs and boxes that we decorated with autumn leaves, pumpkins, and sunflowers. Finally, in one second, we managed to get the perfect picture!

Happy Halloween from Prada's Bunch!

After that, we had a family reunion for every major holiday. Christmas, Easter, Mother's Day, etc. It was entertaining to have them all together. It was such a special post for our friends. They marveled in the amazing work Lulu, Lily Chanel's mom, and I did. It took us hours, but we did it! From 2015 to 2020 we took many family pictures.

Our first family Christmas picture was one of the most cherished family Christmas photos we ever took. The puppies were almost a year old. Sitting amongst Christmas Trees and presents with their red scarfs… I was so proud of all of them! They truly looked like the magnificent dogs they are.

In 2016, I decided that I wanted to make calendars! I had so many amazing pictures. I decided to donate the proceeds to a non-kill dog rescue and a golden retriever rescue. I also made Christmas ornaments with their Christmas pictures. All the proceeds were added to the calendar donation. It made me so happy to see pictures of all of the beautiful Christmas Trees of our friends with our precious puppies in them.

The calendars took a lot of time, and they were incredibly detailed work. Setting up everything, the design, the printing, the sales. But I made it happen! I knew they were loved and cherished by anyone who got them. At the end, they were a labor of love.

And our followers did not disappoint! They were thrilled to have a little piece of Prada's Bunch with them. Our first calendar was for the year 2017. It was a recollection of the puppies' first year of life.

Each year the calendars had a different theme. All of them had many pictures and a little story about what was going on with the dogs that month. It was a marvel to see them grow each month and see how they developed their own personalities.

Our Journey of Love and Adventure

Our friends proudly sent pictures of the calendars on the walls of their homes and offices. My heart was so happy. It was a way to express love and gratitude. I even sent a box to my dear sister-in-law Dannia and my brother, Beto, in Atlanta, GA. She had a wonderful time selling them at their donut shop, Dough in the Box.

Someone asked me once why I took the time to take pictures and post Prada's Bunch adventures every day. I said I wanted to share the joy I felt watching them grow. Life is so fragile and hard, and a lot of times, sadness is at our door. Sometimes, by scrolling on Facebook, you find someone or something funny that makes you smile. In our case, people found our posts and saw adorable golden puppies being cute or getting into mischief. It brought a smile to their faces and a happy moment to their hearts. At that very same moment, their minds were somewhere else and for a few minutes they forgot their own suffering and despair.

I saw my friends on the street that followed us, and they would all say how happy they were when they saw the puppies.

So many people have told me that the first thing they do when they open Facebook is to look for my post every morning. That is priceless. All the comments on each post saying that they love and cherish us are priceless.

I learned that we have friends from all over the world. United Kingdom, India, Belgium, Canada, France, Portugal, Ireland, Spain, Australia, and other parts of Europe, South America, many cities in the United States, and many local friends.

The fact that we can read a comment from Corine from Belgium or connect with Becky in Minnesota, Mona in the Northwest Territories in Canada, and so many others... People who, by now, are family. We exchanged comments and even became incredibly good friends and liked each other's private page. They are my friends now. I care about them as they care about me and my family. People I have never met in person but that have supported me in so many ways. In the good and in the bad.

It is worth the time. If you are reading this, thank you for letting me and my bunch into your life and make a difference in it.

Prada's Bunch and Friends followers were and are family. To this day, we have more than 4,000 followers on Facebook and a little more than 2,000 on Instagram.

Our followers were confirmation that we were delivering happiness through a screen. They were the steady calm in our storm. The storm that I never knew could come. But it did. In the most heartbreaking way possible.

Chapter 7

*"There have been times when fear crippled all my senses.
I let the tears run but did not withhold my footsteps."*
— **Abhijit Naskar**

Prada and the Unthinkable

Life was great!

We went to the cabin for New Years. We had so much fun running around the mountain and celebrating their first birthday there. My parents were there with Ruby and part of the celebration.

Happy Birthday Prada's Bunch!!! ♡🎉🍰🎂♡ We so much **enjoyed celebrating!!!** 🎂Thanks to my parents and great friends **that made this awesome birthday possible!!** ♡ The kids were not too convinced about the commotion, so the cake had to come to their level 😋 Grandma spoiled them silly!!! Yummy cake all around!! ♡🎂♡🎂♡🎂

My mom had the best time giving cake to all the dogs. She loved to spoil them so much! She was so happy.

The post went viral! Hundreds of messages and so much love for the bunch.

I felt emotional thinking about the entire year we just had and posted this for our friends:

Our Journey of Love and Adventure

Personal Note:

As I had the chance to read and like (I hope all 🖤🐶) of your beautiful and heartfelt birthday messages to the kids, I cannot help but feel overwhelmed and blessed to receive so many beautiful wishes for them. THANK YOU! 🖤🎂

We are so lucky to have the chance to share with you, our marvelous group of friends, our journey. You have been such an integral part in raising Prada's Bunch. Your love, encouragement, support and even the occasional reprimand for mischief, have been wonderful in pushing me to make them better dogs. I constantly talk about our page and all of you! 🐶 I think my real-life friends may be a little bored already lol but that is ok. I understand not everyone loves dogs as much as I do. Not only because they are dogs, but what they represent.

We have many plans for the next year. I want them to finish their training and have them behave well so we can move on to our next mission. I hope and pray we can become therapy dogs so we can give even more help and love to many. I want to keep raising money for the rescue shelters by making and selling things with Prada's Bunch pictures, like we did with the Christmas ornaments and the calendars. God gave me the opportunity to help. By sharing through this page, making things, etc. I feel honored and I hope He gives me the strength and courage to get everything done as I want. Thanks to ALL OF YOU 🖤 you are so special. I hope you keep visiting us and enjoy what will be an exciting first year! 🎉🎊 Happy 2016! 🎊🐾 May you receive many blessings! Love, Silvia and Prada.

Our friends expressed the same sentiment! They had a wonderful time watching the dogs grow. Our adventures were the highlight of their day. They were always telling others about what Prada and the kids were doing. Such a special love.

The puppies were officially one year old and now less puppies and instead, amazing, beautiful golden retriever teenagers the same size as their mom and taller than Uncle Spiky. Which still did not matter to Spiky, Uncle Spiky aka "The Boss." They respected and adored him.

The human kids were growing too. Going to school and doing their after-school activities. Life was getting complicated. We kept posting and sharing our lives on our Facebook page with love, humor, and shenanigans.

Charlie and Lalique started their obedience classes again. They had one when Jack was home and Prada went too to show off her command skills. It was so much fun watching their little minds trying to figure out what to do.

They were so smart and so naughty too. Especially Lalique. She had a whole fan club all to herself. They were the most dedicated group of defenders ever. It was never her fault. She was full of mischief and usually the protagonist and instigator of their shenanigans. Charlie Brown was a sweet dog with soulful eyes and did everything his sister did.

Mami Prada was always next to me and keeping an eye on the kids. Like the good Mami she was. Their relationship was better too. They accepted each other and they respected the time Mami Prada and I would have together.

We kept our traditional posts going. Good morning and good night, birthday posts, pool time, "you are so grounded" posts, which were frequent to the delight of their fan club.

Prada loved Carlos so much, too. She would spend a lot of time with him in his room. They would lay down on the bed and Carlos would give her lots of belly rubs. One night he felt something different in her belly. He called me and showed it to me. It was a little mass on one of her nipples. I did not really think much of it. Thankfully, we were going to the vet the next day to take Spiky and her in for their checkup.

Spiky turned 11 years old on January 19, 2016. Time was flying for my old grumpy dog. I was concerned because he had some issues with his eye too.

On January 26, 2016, we went to see Dr. Carmen Vazquez. Prada loved her! But also knew that she was there to be checked out. She used to hide behind me, probably thinking "if I hide Dr. Vazquez cannot see me." Dr. Vazquez loved them both so much and was very patient with them. She checked out Spiky and gave him the vaccines and performed the usual health check. He was in top shape for an 11-year-old Shih Tzu. The kids kept him young!

It was time to check Prada.

Dr. Vazquez checked her ears and performed her regular health check as well. All seem ok. I mentioned that we found something in particular in one of her nipples. Dr. Vazquez checked her out and looked at me.

"I am so worried about this," she said.

"Why," I responded.

"This is a tumor. I want to remove it now," she said, increasingly frantic. "We need to have a biopsy of this mass ASAP."

I was speechless. What was going on! I did not understand! Prada is happy and healthy. How? Why? What is happening!

At that very moment Dr. Vazquez left the room and cancelled the rest of her appointments. She got her staff briefed and prepared for surgery. I took Spiky home and came back to wait for Prada to get out of surgery.

Dr. Vazquez proceeded to remove the tumor. After the surgery she told me that she did not like what she saw. We needed to wait for the results. It may take a week.

I called Miguel and burst into tears. Our precious Prada might have Cancer. I could not believe this.

With a big lump in my throat and shaky hands, I posted the news. I told them I was waiting for her. So many messages came through. The post had hundreds of comments. They could not believe it either. They were in shock! They were praying! "We love you Mami Prada. Be strong! You will make it."

Prada finally was alert and able to leave the clinic. I cried with her head on my lap the whole drive home.

I told her then, "Prada. We will get through this. You will be okay. You are loved and so beautiful. Nothing bad will happen. I will take care of you. I will save you."

Our biggest nightmare was confirmed February 1, 2016. I received the call from Dr.

Vazquez. With tears in her voice, she said, "I am so sorry. We got the report from the lab. The mass is cancerous and extremely aggressive. It can metastasize to other organs through the lymph nodes. We need to act fast to save Prada."

Diagnosis: Tubuloalveolar carcinoma.

My world shattered. How is this possible? My sweet Prada. My beautiful dog. We went through so much with the puppies. We fought destiny to save them. Now she was sick. Why God?

But we humans cannot question God. We simply must have faith. I had faith in God to guide my thoughts, my prayers, and my actions. I saved the puppies. I will save Mami Prada.

I got a grip on my emotions. And called Dr. Vazquez.

"We must save Prada; she is only four years old. What do we do now?"

Dr. Vazquez had already found a couple of animal oncologists and gave me their numbers. I called one and made the appointment. On Saturday of that same week, we went to see the new doctor.

Miguel was with me, and we walked in with Prada. We provided our information and waited for the doctor to come to the room.

She came into the room with tons of facts and statistics. She said plain and simple, "The tumor is extremely aggressive. She will last not more than a year even if she gets treatment. The cancer has likely metastasized already. We can do chemo, but it will not save her."

Prada was next to me. Laying down on the floor. Head down. The doctor did not even look at her. I looked at Miguel and we both nodded. I said "Thank you. We will call you back with our decision."

We left feeling hopeless and speechless. We got in the car and cried together with Mami Prada's face between us. We both agreed that this was not the answer. We would not accept this outcome. There must be someone that can save Prada.

Another call to Dr. Vazquez and she agreed with us. She mentioned another place where we could go.

Another appointment and this time we got a better response but with extremely aggressive treatment. They wanted to do a surgery where they would remove both sets of mamma glands and lymph nodes. This was extremely expensive. The first quote was on the high side of $15,000.00. I was devastated. First, that the surgery was so intense and there was no guarantee that Prada was going to be okay afterwards, and second, the expense. I never thought of getting insurance for her. And that was a big lesson I learned after all that was going on. We had a few savings that were being used to pay for the first surgery.

What do I do now?

I posted on our page the situation. They were very much invested in Prada and all that we were going through. They needed to know what was happening. They sent messages of hope and love. I was so grateful for their support.

A friend of mine, Cat, told me that she took her cats to this wonderful doctor in Fort Lauderdale. His practice consisted of all kinds of specialties for animals. Oncology included. She trusted him. I needed someone to trust. I made an appointment.

On Monday morning I got Prada in the car and drove one hour to the hospital. After giving our information they took us to a room.

I will never forget the face of this beautiful doctor. She came in with a big kind smile on her face and passed me on her way to Prada. She threw

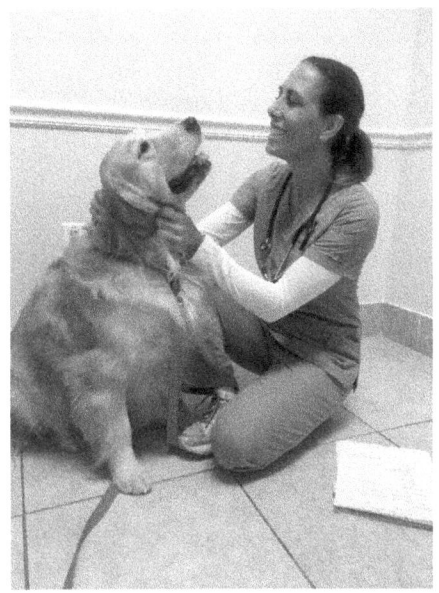
herself on the floor and got tons of kisses and love from Prada. Her name is Dr. Lisa DiBernardi. She is Italian and genuine. She loved Prada at first sight! Both her name and her kisses. Dr. DiBernardi was a long-time owner of golden retrievers. She knew. She had gone through this.

Right there and then, I looked up and said, "Thank you, God." We are in good hands. I trust we will save Mami Prada. A weight lifted from my heart.

We proceeded to talk about the best plan for Prada. She would have the surgeon remove the side of the mamma glands where the tumor was found as well as the lymph nodes. This was a more conservative approach than the previous doctor. After she recuperates from the surgery, we would start chemotherapy. She would have six rounds. One every three weeks. This will help prevent the development of more cancer cells. Chemo is hard. There are secondary effects. But it is the best alternative. We needed to make sure she was clear. If all goes according to plan, Prada would be in remission, and she would have many years left with us. Those were the words I needed to hear!

We got the appointment for surgery. We needed to get ready for all that was coming — the surgery was significant and very delicate. The financial liability was getting bigger, and my strength was wavering, I knew I had a mountain to climb. I needed to keep it together. I had my family to take care of, the puppies, on top of the difficulties of everyday life. There was a long road ahead of us.

We got in the car, and I took a big breath and looked Prada in her eyes. I said, "We got this Prada. I will not let you down." She licked my face and laid her head on my lap, as if she were saying "I know mom. I know you will."

That night I posted about our visit. I explained the plan and how blessed we were to find this amazing doctor in our path. How difficult it was to hear the diagnosis again and what could happen. How worried I was that I had some savings, but I was not completely sure how much in the end it would all cost. How thankful I was that Dr. Vazquez was unconditional and never questioned the chance to save Mami Prada. I will forever be in her debt. Now Dr. DiBernardi and her team were the angels in charge.

The comments were amazing and so full of love and support. Words of encouragement, prayers and some even talked about their own experiences. It was special to feel their love. There was no doubt that they cared. They saw Prada as one of their own and wished nothing but good health and best wishes. It was a very emotional post. I cried so much reading each of the comments. My heart was full of gratitude.

Many of our friends wanted to help financially. They wanted to send me money to pay for the vet bills. I was flabbergasted, since never in my life had I thought to receive money from complete strangers even though I continually recognized their names and comments on each post, I did not think that was an option. I was incredibly grateful and apologetic. I do not think I could do that. They insisted and really persisted. They loved her and thought of her like she was one of their own, they felt the need to help. I said I would think of something. I was not going to take their money without giving them something in return.

I wanted to hug them and to cry in their arms. I felt in my bones their generosity. I was so blessed to have my family's support and all the amazing people of Prada's Bunch.

During one of the visits to the oncology office, I saw this sign posted. I fought extremely hard with my emotions, so I did not crumble right there after I read it. Not only for Prada and all the fur kids fighting this fight. But for all of us that may be going through a treatment, may have a family member or friend fighting this battle too.

What Cancer Cannot Do

Cancer is so limited.......

It cannot cripple love,

It cannot shatter hope,

It cannot corrode faith,

It cannot destroy peace,

It cannot destroy confidence,

It cannot kill friendship,

It cannot suppress memories,

It cannot silence courage,

It cannot invade the soul,

It cannot steal eternal life,

It cannot conquer the spirit,

-Author Unknown

The last line. "Cancer cannot conquer the spirit." It certainly cannot. And certainly, not ours. I promised to keep posting about the kids and their adventures, birthdays celebrations, and all their mischief.

Our followers knew when they scrolled their Facebook feed, they would see our everyday posts of "Good Morning" and "Good Night."

Our purpose in life can come disguised in many ways. We had an incredibly special one and that was to keep our dear friends smiling and wondering about what Lalique and Charlie could do next. They needed to see Mami Prada smile and Uncle Spiky's grumpy face.

I did that not only for their benefit. But for myself. I was so worried. Posting about our day was my lifeline. It made me remember that I was not alone. I had my family and my Prada's Bunch friends. We shared an amazing journey of love and adventure.

Now it was time to save Prada. We had a plan.

Chapter 8

"Dogs die. But dogs live, too. Right up until they die, they live. They live brave, beautiful lives. They protect their families. And love us, and make our lives a little brighter, and they do not waste time being afraid of tomorrow."
– **Dan Gemeinhart**

Prada's Bunch and Friends' Support Came With Faith, Hope, and Love

It was the day of the surgery, February 23, 2016. We left early in the morning to drive to the clinic. I was so scared and praying so hard. Our friends were all glued to Facebook waiting for news.

We got to the clinic and met with the surgeon, Dr. Bibevski. Prada was a little anxious and was wondering what was going on. She hid behind me as she always did when we visited a vet office.

We had a little alone time before she had to go. I gave her tons of kisses and hugs, and she licked me right back. I knew she was in the best hands and that with everyone's prayers she was covered in love and strength.

It was time to go. I saw her walking away and my tears were flowing down my cheeks. My heart was so sad but at the same time, so hopeful. I needed to be strong for Mami Prada.

I had to leave, with a heavy heart, and go back home to Miami because they told me they would have to keep her overnight to monitor her. I drove all the way home with my prayers. I had never been apart from her, it was so hard.

One of the followers created this hashtag **#pradastrong**. It was perfect. Prada is strong and she will show that to the world.

I was able to share this update later:

UPDATE ON PRADA:

Thanks to God and all the wonderful prayers, love, and demonstration of love♡

Prada is out of surgery and doing great!! Dr. Bibevski did not "see" evidence of more cancer; however, we need to wait for the results in three to five days. She was able to clean the tumor area and remove the lymph node. Based on those results, we will determine with the oncologist a chemotherapy treatment. ♡ **Thank you, God, for this beautiful blessing!!** ♡🙏**#pradastrong**

This post went viral. Many people liked it and commented. Wonderful words of love and encouragement.

I kept dealing with normal life during the day taking care of the human kids and the furry ones. Spiky was looking for Prada everywhere. He knew something was amiss.

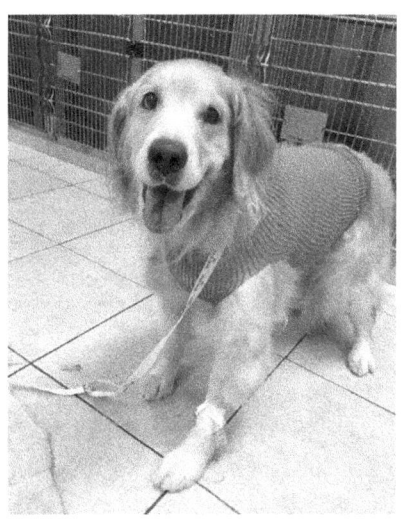

At night, I called the clinic, and the nurse told me that Prada woke up and was in good spirits. She stood up, went potty and ate a bit. That was such special and wonderful news. The nurse sensed how worried I was and how much love I had for Prada, that she went out of the way to reassure me Prada was well. She said, "I will email you something I need you to see." To my surprise was a picture of Prada!!! Her sweet face smiling!!! Still a bit unsteady with her big eyes and her blue dressing covering her body. It was the most precious picture I have seen in a while!

Of course, I shared it with our friends. They were so happy to see Mami Prada. It was like looking at our own heart! A blessing that felt so real!

Mami Prada was okay.

My beautiful girl ♡ thank God she is doing well. Always smiling. God bless her. (Excuse me while I get my tissue paper) I have been strong but now it is time to let the tears go. Good night, friends! ♡ Thank you so much for the prayers, love and support ♡ God bless you all.

It was overwhelming to read hundreds of messages, feeling so much love. Prada was theirs too and we cried and prayed together.

Throughout the next day, I kept posting updates. I went to pick her up in the afternoon. My son Carlos went with me to help her get in the car. He was also very emotional and happy to see Mami Prada.

Prada was waiting for us with this beautiful smile, like a ray of sunshine in the morning! We got instructions on how to take care of the incision, give her medication, etc. Finally, it was time to go home. Our precious girl was on the mend.

It was incredibly special to experience the love and prayers that everyone expressed to us. Do you think it is possible to feel it through the screen? I did. I really did. Every word of encouragement, kindness, love, worry, advice I felt them in my heart.

When we got home, Spiky and the kids were so excited! I had to do my best to keep them calm so not to hurt Prada. After a bit, they all settled next to her. Mami Prada was home. Now we are complete.

The next day Prada was feeling the pain of the incision. It was natural due to the kind of surgery she had. The surgeon cut from the top of her chest all the way down. I did not even know how many stitches there were. It was huge. I was grateful that Prada was able to walk and go potty. Her meals were a little tricky. She did not want to eat her regular food. I prepared chicken and rice for her, and she ate that. Thankfully, it helped her to get some strength back.

We got mail! There were lots of greeting cards and some even sent gift cards for me to get toys and treats for Mami Prada and the kids. I was so touched and grateful for all the willingness to help. There are still good generous people in the world, and we were so lucky to have them as part of Prada's Bunch.

One night I was looking at my phone and at all the pictures I had since the puppies were born. At that moment I saw the possibilities! I knew what I was going to make! After some thought, I found something I could offer in return for the money people wanted to send to me to pay for the medical bills. It would take time and lots of creativity. Thankfully, I am a creative person and always loved to make homemade gifts for my kids' teachers. An idea was brewing in my mind! I can make something beautiful and something that our friends could cherish.

I created a series of "Prada's Bunch Cards of Love."

I selected the best pictures I had. The plan was to make greeting cards. I ordered ivory plain cards 5 x 7 with envelopes. I got stamps with messages, ink, ribbons, and tons of glue!

I created cards with the pictures on the front. A stamped message in the back. Blank inside for a personalized message.

I had puppy cards, birthday cards, Christmas cards, Halloween cards, every holiday! Even funny cards and pool party cards. I made 240 samples! I was ready to sell them and raise money to pay for our Prada's treatment.

Our friends loved the idea! I posted a sample, and they went crazy! Yes! I want them! I love them! They are perfect! I was so happy! And so relieved.

I posted each group of cards, and they emailed me their selection. They were so happy to get their cards and help! I created a system and worked every night until the early hours. I wanted to make sure that everyone received their order.

It was an intense few months. Working day and night, taking care of Prada and the kids. Posting our usual shenanigans and updates. I made each card with so much love and care. I wrapped them with a special ribbon. They were a labor of love and gratitude.

I shipped them all over the world! I made a special order for a friend named Mona; she bought the whole collection — 240 cards. She lives in the Northwest Territories in Canada. Honestly, I had never even heard of that area. See, that is the beauty of social media as we can connect with people all around the world. I sent cards to all parts of United States, to India, London, Belgium, and so many other countries. To be honest, I did not really care about the postage cost. For me, it was all about giving back something special for all the love and support we received.

And just like that, I sold about 1,000 cards. Many people sent more money than the cards were worth, I was astonished about how generous they all were. They got their orders and were delighted. They absolutely loved to have with them a little remembrance of Prada and her puppies.

On March 1, 2016, I posted this special update:

UPDATE ON PRADA

Dear Friends, I want to THANK GOD for this beautiful blessing and THANK YOU for all the love and prayers. The support. The worries. The messages. The tears and the joy. I thank you from my heart! ♡🙏 and mami Prada and the kids join in gratitude as well. ♡👶👶👶👶

PRADA's results are NEGATIVE! 👍👏👏👏♡🙏 no cancer cells were found on the tissues removed nor in the lymph node. Isn't it awesome?!!!♡😃

There were residuals from the first tumor that were removed. But nothing significant that could regenerate fast.

The plan is still as discussed before. She will receive chemotherapy to eliminate, finally, those nasty cells that may be floating in her bloodstream. 👍The chemotherapy starts March 14. Then every three weeks thereafter I must take her again. For a total of six rounds. I will take it day by day. So far, I know my family and I have done the right thing and helped her have an incredibly good life with her kids and us. We still have many adventures to enjoy together!!! ♡☺

Again, I do not have enough words to say what my heart feels now. But know for sure that I love you all and have you in my prayers always. You are all family. Blessings! ♡ #pradastrong

That post was a blessing and a relief to all!

Tons of comments, kind words, blessings, happy tears, tons of hearts and smiley faces! The best news in a long time!

Now we keep fighting. The second side of the treatment was about to start.

As humans, dogs also get secondary effects from chemotherapy. It is brutal. The drugs are strong and sometimes they do not work. We had faith that this treatment would work, and that Prada was going to survive.

While we were waiting for the chemo to start, I kept working on the cards. I already mailed several of them. I received tons of messages with pictures. They said that they loved them! How special they are! They truly cherished them. Some said they would not give them away! They wanted to treasure them. I felt immense gratitude when I saw all those comments.

I printed the pictures at the local Walgreens. The gentleman working at the photo station loved the dogs and was so excited to receive an order from me. He even looked for extra coupons so that I could use them to get cheaper prints.

I had so many angels around me! I was truly blessed in this time of need.

I met so many special people through Prada's Bunch. One of them is my dear friend Becky. She made these beautiful coffee mugs with gold letters that spelled "Love" and even made some with our hashtag #pradastrong.

The day before I took Prada for her first chemotherapy, I posted this message:

personal note: LABOR OF LOVE

I would like to take the chance to express my eternal gratitude to a wonderful, hardworking, unselfish woman and friend, Becky Potts. THANK YOU.

You are one of the most amazing people I have ever met on Facebook. One day you saw my worry and my struggle, and without hesitation, without a thought of profit or personal gain, you jumped in and offered your "labor of love" to help mami Prada.

As the stamp says, *"God doesn't look at how much we do, but with how much love we do it."* Mother Teresa

You, my friend, just won His grace with this deed.

You took your time and resources and created by hand every single cup. And to top it off you even pleased our dear friends with their personal requests.

Not to mention your kindness in upgrading the shipping so they could receive their cups as soon as possible. You are amazing. And I am happy and proud to call you, my friend. May God return to you every single act of kindness in love, health, and prosperity.

To all my dear friends who bought a cup, THANK YOU. You have in your hands not just a cup. But again, a labor of love. From Becky, who made it, to you who gave your money to help. May you always remember the love this represents.

You are all a blessing to me. Mami Prada and I are so fortunate to be able to receive such a generous contribution.

I want to make it clear that every cent that Becky sends to me will be put towards Prada's chemotherapy treatments. Each treatment costs about $600. We need to do at least six of them.

This contribution helps so much.

Not to mention the generosity of some that also are buying the handmade cards I am making. ♡♡♡🙏

I am fortunate to have the means to support my family, but this is a huge expense that I never thought I would have to incur. You all know my dedication to Prada's Bunch. They mean the world

to me, and I know you love them as your own. I am infinitely grateful for that.

May God bless you always.

With love, Silvia

The day arrived. March 14, 2016. The day for Prada's first chemotherapy. I was so worried. What if this treatment is too hard on her? What if this is not what she needs? Should I not do it? So many questions in my mind and heart. But I trusted God. He placed in our journey great doctors, and I trusted them. Here we go.

The night before I posted that Mami Prada was going to wear an orange shirt for her chemotherapy. Prada always wore orange color bandanas and bows. She looked beautiful!

This orange shirt had her name "Mami Prada" in the front and "#PradaStrong" in the back.

This is the t-shirt Mami Prada will wear tomorrow to go to her first chemotherapy treatment 🤍🙏

I would like to add the names of all the friends that love her and pray for her ♡ if you would like your name written in her t shirt, please make a comment and I will add it. Tomorrow morning, she will wear her "armor of love and prayer." Thank you ♡🙏 blessings!! #pradastrong

It got 192 comments — 192 names were on her shirt. With hundreds more that I added later.

This became indeed her "Armor of Love and Prayer."

She wore this T-shirt for all her six chemo visits. The doctors and nurses were in awe to see how many people loved Prada. What a blessing to experience that.

Every time, it hit me. This is real. This is the Power of Love.

We arrived at the clinic for her first chemotherapy. Dr. DiBernardi and her assistant Tiffany greeted us and took Prada with them. And my heart too.

I waited in the lobby and after two hours, Mami Prada came running towards me. Smiling and wagging her tail. She did amazing. Her vitals were good through the chemo, and she was in good spirits. Time to go home and rest.

When we got home after our one-hour drive, she was not feeling so good. She did not want to eat. That is not normal for a golden. They are always hungry and Mami Prada was no different. But she refused to eat. No vomit or diarrhea. Just a bit quiet and keeping mostly to herself. I gave her a pill for nausea and tried again to feed her. She did not want to eat her food. Only if I fed her human food, like turkey. I know she ate it to please me. Bless her heart. The doctor said that may happen.

I decided that it was better to feed her chicken and rice. Food that she liked very much. I researched a bit about this process. Seems to be that they associate their dry food with nausea. We know the food is not the cause. But they believe so. They do not want to eat it. That is why when you offer food with a good smell like chicken, they change their attitude. Also, they recommend changing their bowl and even the place where they eat. It is interesting to see how their system works. I did all that and Mami Prada started to eat again.

Life was still sailing along. Some days were good. Some were not good. But all were blessed. I was exhausted. So much work, the stress of having Mami Prada sick, the responsibility I had to make all the cards and ship them too. I rarely took a break. Our whole family was taking care of Prada. Uncle Spiky and the kids were never far. We were in this together.

All was well. I learned to live with all of it. Prada was on the mend and the kids were still being silly and making me laugh. We celebrated Saint Patrick's Day with their sisters Ruby and Lily Chanel. Our pictures were so special! They were already familiar with the process. Charlie Brown was the most precious leprechaun! It was a great distraction to plan our photoshoots.

Our Prada's Bunch friends never missed a post! Tons of likes and sweet comments with encouraging words that gave me strength.

On the day I was getting Prada ready for her last chemo, I found something weird on her back paw. A mass on one of her toes. What is this? This cannot be. We were on the home stretch. Dear God. What now?

Another challenge got in our way...

Chapter 9

"It's not the size of the dog in the fight, it's the size of the fight in the dog."
Mark Twain

Veni, Vidi, Vici – I came, I saw, I conquered

It was time to go to our sixth chemotherapy appointment for Prada. It was June 6, 2016. I was afraid of what having that mass on her toe meant. Did she need another surgery? What if they needed to amputate her toe? What are the possibilities of having it removed? More chemotherapy, more suffering? Was I strong enough emotionally to handle another crisis? I had no choice but to confront it and do my best.

When we got to the clinic, Dr. Dibernardi decided to stop her current treatment. It was not recommended to continue with it if we could not identify what was on her toe. Unfortunately, Dr. Bibevski, her surgeon, was on a two-week vacation and her next appointment was a month away. Dr. Dibernardi took a sample for biopsy. We needed to get results to determinate what was the best path to take.

We went home sad and defeated. We needed to delay her treatment and get the results of the biopsy then decide.

Our spirits were a little crushed. But with all the love and support from our Prada's Bunch and our family, we decided not to let this stop us from getting Mami Prada strong and healthy. We kept loving her and living our lives. Lots of mischief and plenty of posts.

I also had a scare with my little girl Lalique. She had a problem with her right eye. A trip to see Dr. Vazquez and we confirmed it was entropion. A condition that some dogs suffer when the lashes grow towards the inside of the eye. Thankfully, I had a little break with Prada and took care of Lalique. She had surgery and was the prettiest patient ever. She had this huge cone on her. I decorated it with colored flowers and stickers. Prada's Bunch fan club was worried but also happy that she was on the mend and with a very stylish cone of shame.

Our Journey of Love and Adventure

On July 14, 2016, we had an appointment to come back to see the doctor and figure out our next course of action.

This was my post for that day.

"Today's visit was to finally decide about the mass on her toe. The biopsy was unclear. They could not be 100% certain that it was a mast tumor.

We had three options. Leave it and monitor it, remove the mass, and have another biopsy, and the last option was to amputate the toe and remove the mass to eliminate any risk.

These options were in my mind and my heart for the two weeks it took Dr. Bibevski to come back from vacation. I knew that leaving it was not the option. The other two were quite different and determinant decisions. I always try to be fair and give science a chance. You know all that we have been through and submitting her to an amputation without a 100% certainly was not my preference. And not my heart option either. Thank God it was not what her doctors, both oncologist and surgeon, agreed should be done.

We all agreed to remove the mass and have another biopsy. It is a simple surgery. Prada will not have too much down time and she will have all her precious toes.

This surgery is tomorrow morning. Yes. We need to do it as fast as possible because we want the biopsy results on Tuesday which is her LAST CHEMO!!! 👍♡🙏 so that will give Dr DiBernardi an idea of the medicine to use for the chemo. We will be done on Tuesday! God willing!!!

Also, today we had a blood test to check her thyroid. Her fur is coarse, and her pretty tail is very slim. But this is not something to be concerned about. With some medicine, she would be back to her pretty self.

Yes, my dear friends. I am relieved. I am happy and looking forward to telling you that our Precious Mami Prada is cancer free! 👏👏👏👏❤️🙏

Your love and prayers and the financial support has been a blessing to us.

I cannot find enough words of gratitude. Only to wish you all back many blessings and the best of love and health.

My prayers are with you all! Love, Silvia

The love and support were overwhelming. So many comments to wish for a successful surgery. Prayers sent!

After we got home, we celebrated Miguel's birthday! We had pizza and delicious cake! Prada was the first one on a chair expecting a huge piece of vanilla cake. Miguel was happy to celebrate and share his day with Prada and the great news!

The next day was a day I was not ready for but brought so much wonder and gratitude to my heart.

When I got to the clinic with Prada in her amazing beautiful "Armor of Love and Prayers" orange shirt the staff welcomed me with amazing news.

Someone called and donated $500 towards Prada's medical bills. This person wanted to be anonymous. I felt relieved, loved, and so humbled. My heart was full of gratitude. This donation helped me so much. I posted my most sincere thank you to this Angel lady that made such a generous gift to us. Later, I found out who it was and got to talk to her. She did it on behalf of her daughter that she lost very suddenly. She loved animals and her mom thought it was an honor to donate to help such a beautiful dog. We were honored to receive that help.

It was time for Mami Prada to go with the nurse and get her toe mass removed. I waited for her with much anticipation. What if something else was there? Or her toe could not be saved? So many questions. But I was relieved when hours later, she came walking back with Prada smiling and a bag covering the bandage on her back paw. My heart melted right there. I was so relieved.

Time to go home my dear Prada. Tomorrow will be another day.

Meanwhile, my fundraising efforts increased. I created other items to sell. I made two different t-shirts, totes, notebooks with pictures, bookmarks. Our friends at Prada's Bunch absolutely loved them and were immensely proud to wear and use all the items. I am not sure how I did it all. I planned, scheduled, ordered, made some of the items, packed, and shipped all during the nights and weekends. I was busy as a bee. I needed to do it. It gave me a purpose. I was committed to return the blessings we received.

My mom always told me that a grateful heart will conquer all. No matter your circumstances, be grateful. Be a fighter and never give up. Her words will always be part of my own conviction and ethical work. My mom was my greatest supporter. She bought everything too! I was blessed to have her by my side. She was Prada's favorite person after me.

We received so many beautiful cards for Mami Prada. All with the most amazing and loving messages. We even got some of ours back with special messages! I have a window in my kitchen, and I kept their pictures, all the amazing cards, and gifts we had received. It was my happy window full of love.

I remember one day; we received a little box from an incredibly special friend. In this box were about 10 baby socks and a note. It said "this is to cover Mami Prada's paw so she can always have it clean and healthy" I love you Mami Prada, love, J.

How special to know that this person took the time and the effort to send this. It is an extraordinarily strong bond we do have with the animals we love. Even if they are not ours or live far away. We are blessed to be the recipient of so much kindness.

On July 19, 2016, I got Mami Prada ready for her last chemotherapy. This was the last trip to receive this treatment that affected Prada in so many ways. Her coat, her pretty tail was almost gone, the hair around her eyes was gone. Her appetite was inconsistent, and she was eating because I sat with her, and every day I hand fed her food.

This was also my day. It was a milestone in my efforts. I promised Mami Prada I would save her. I did that. I promised her I would not give up. And I never did.

This was my post to our Prada's Bunch Friends that day.

When Prada was diagnosed with mammal gland cancer in January, my world was tilted. Big time. I was told I needed to get her to an oncologist. Fast. The tumor which her vet removed in an emergency surgery was extremely aggressive.

Our Journey of Love and Adventure

That is how we came to be at this oncology vet office.

I never went inside while she was having chemo. I never asked to go in. I do not think I could have seen it anyway. But they said she was the best. I took the chance while she was inside and brought snacks for the staff. And took pictures of mami Prada and them.

Today was our last chemotherapy visit and we brought a gift. I made a collage of all their pictures and their smiles. You can see love and compassion. Care and commitment. They absolutely love what they do. We are so grateful to be able to show what an amazing team they are. I hope this gives a little reassurance to new patients coming with their heart hurting and wanting to help their beautiful pet. I hope it reassures them they are well cared for.

Mami Prada's smiles give hope, peace, and love.

Thank you, dear friends of Lauderdale Vet Specialist, for saving mami Prada and giving her a chance to enjoy life a little longer and a little better if God will want.

And thank you, all of you. My dear friends for coming along for each trip. Each comment, each prayer, and beautiful thoughts helped me endure those hours of waiting for Prada.

I wish I could say Mami Prada is Cancer Free. As of now she is. And that is good enough. ♡🙏 May God bless her.

Love you, Many Blessings

Silvia

We had an amazing and beautiful farewell from the doctors and the staff. They loved the collage of pictures. It was truly special. I worked on it for many days. Printing the pictures and finding the right spot for each picture. They placed the collage in one of the rooms. I hope that people who visit the clinic can feel reassured that they are in the right place.

While we gave the gift to Dr. DiBernardi and Tiffany, her assistant, they sat on each side of Prada. There is this picture that I will never forget. It is so beautiful and special.... Can you see the love? Each of them turned towards Prada and gave her a kiss at the same time. It was such a happy picture! How blessed we were to have that. I would forever be grateful to God for that amazing blessing.

On August 30, 2016. We came back for a final checkup. After this, her Vet, Dr. Vazquez, could continue the follow-ups and make sure all was in order.

This was my post on that special day:

THANK YOU, GOD, 🎉👍♡🙈 Mami Prada is a success! She is in remission!! ♡🙏Bless her beautiful soul! X-rays, ultrasound, and examination look clear.

♡ By the way! I am incredibly grateful for the amazing and understanding staff. We brought an apple pie as a gift, which Prada, in her rush to get out of the car, stepped on🐶 thankfully, everybody enjoyed it regardless of that misspawed episode 😊♡🐾

Oh! I love how our gift of pictures is displayed! ♡♡♡ #pradastrong ♡ #blessed #kickedcancerbutt

This post went viral! More than 100 comments. All full of gratitude and love. Some said they were crying with joy. They were so happy! Fantastic! This is awesome! Our prayers were answered!

Veni, Vidi, Vici – I Came, I Saw, I Conquered

Mami Prada was ready to keep living her beautiful life full of amazing moments and so many blessings.

October is Breast Cancer awareness month. Since Prada had mammary cancer, it constitutes breast cancer in a dog.

On October 15, 2016, we organized a walkathon in honor of Prada and all the doggies that had suffered or were going through treatment for the same cancer.

Everyone from Prada's Bunch that was able from around the world and in United States joined us. The only condition was that they needed to wear something orange to support Prada's armor of love and prayer.

I received so many messages with pictures of people and their dogs walking and sending loving messages of support. It was an extraordinary part of our journey. I will forever be grateful to all the people that participated.

Our life, after all we went through, became a little less stressful. We were able to be carefree and relaxed. Mami Prada was feeling great. Her checkups were good. Our Prada's Bunch Friends hit a milestone. 2,000 friends!

We showed love, mischief, shenanigans and tons of pictures and videos.

The dogs were big already and so beautiful. Uncle Spiky had the most adoring fan club. He was cherished for all his grumpiness. Our humans were growing too and becoming independent young adults.

I would close my eyes every night with a grateful prayer.

For Thanksgiving that year we went to the mountains. I was so relieved and exhausted. I needed a break from all. We had such an exciting time! We had the opportunity to just relax and enjoy our beautiful family.

On our way back, we made a special stop. We visited one of the most cherished friends of Prada's Bunch and her family. We went to the house of our friend Rebekah and her husband Daniel in Easley, South Carolina. She had three beautiful goldens as well. One of them, her name is Fenway Belle, is also a cancer survivor like mami Prada. We had a wonderful time talking and being so grateful we were able to meet in person.

On December 31, 2016, I wrote this post:

Mami Prada and I would like to thank you sincerely for all the love, support, prayers, tears, virtual hugs and smiles you gave to us

through the year 2016. We found amazing friends and unbelievable support throughout her cancer journey.

You helped us so much in every way. We appreciate and cherish each like, comment, and message you sent.

We appreciate the prayers. Her "Armor of Love and Prayer" that has all your names represents an amazing symbol of support.

We loved to share with you the puppies' adventures and mischief along the way.

We had many plans. But her health was a priority. Hopefully in 2017 we can start making those plans a reality. Thank you for always being there with a funny comment for their mischievous behaviors, a beautiful wish.

We are humble and immensely proud to be part of your life every time you look for us or we show up to say good morning or good night!

Thank you for getting our calendar. A big stepping stone in Prada's Bunch future. We look forward to every year being able to do this "labor of love" and share it with you.

As this year ends, we wish you all blessings, love, health, and the best this year can bring to each of you and your family!

Thanks for being Prada's Bunch Family! ♡🙏

With love, Silvia and Mami Prada

Little did I know that I was also on my way to finding myself and my most precious gift. Together we conquered. Not only our fears but cancer too, for now.

Chapter 10

"Not all of us can do great things.
But we can do small things with great love."
Mother Teresa

On Our Way to Make a Difference

On January 1, 2017, we celebrated the puppies' second birthday. Their sisters Lily Chanel and Ruby and their brother Jack came to our house for the big celebration! Picture this: six golden retrievers sitting in chairs around a table with birthday hats on, a cake in the middle of the table with candles, and of course, Uncle Spiky also on the table, since he was so small. It was awesome! We had so much fun! The whole family together singing and celebrating. My parents, my sisters, my friend Lulu, and the kids, we all gathered around the dogs singing happy birthday and trying to control the chaos.

Celebrating their birthday was always a huge deal for us. The post from that day was cherished and very much loved. It was the highlight of New Year's Day.

Prada's Bunch two years celebration! 🤍🙏🤍🎉🎂🐶🐶🐶🐶🐶🐶🎉🎂🤍 Ohhh what a family! It is truly a blessing to have a family that loves them as much as I do! It was mayhem!!! 😁 The dogs and humans alike! Definitely a birthday to remember! 🤍🎉🐶🎂

This post went viral. More than 200 comments and 96 shares! Everyone was laughing and enjoying the pictures and videos. Lots of love and Happy Birthday wishes from our Prada's Bunch family.

A few days later, we received an incredibly special box all the way from Belgium from our friend Corine with treats for humans and dogs. Miss

Mona from Canada also sent us gifts, as did Colette from Massachusetts. Many birthday cards too. Prada's Bunch were diehard fans! And we loved them all so much!

The beautiful thing about Prada's Bunch page was that so many people were able to interact with me. They would send messages and through the comments we could connect. People got to know my heart. My abilities to be able to focus and make things happen. The way my heart was so grateful that I would also be willing to help others.

When Prada was having toe mass surgery, I received an incredibly special message from one of our Prada's Bunch friends.

Carrie wrote to me to let me know about an experience she had with one of the students she works with as a therapist for special needs children and as a mental health counselor. This girl was there because she was suffering depression and struggling with herself. Carrie told her about Prada. This girl lit up and said she loved dogs. They were her favorite animal. Carrie then explained that Prada was going through an extremely harsh treatment for cancer. But despite that, Prada was a happy dog. She would smile and wag her tail and jump in the pool and play with her kids. She did not let her struggle dim her light. This girl got it. She understood the message and totally changed her attitude.

I was flabbergasted. How special! That someone by just listening about Prada's journey would recognize love and hope.

Carrie wanted to print copies of Prada's picture to give to the kids. She wanted to ask me if that was okay. I said that I was going to do something even better. I would make the kids little cards of Prada and write in each card a special message. They could keep them in their backpacks, pockets, wallets, etc.

That day I wrote this post:

♡♡ Prada's Bunch Cards of Hope ♡♡

Personal Note:

Prada's Bunch and Friends have been such a blessing to me. That awful day when I left Prada in the vet hospital to have the toe surgery, I received this message. I can only tell you God sent it through this beautiful person. My tears were flowing big time. My spirits were restored a little bit because this gave me the strength to realize that we have, and we can do, so much good for others.

Carrie, one of Prada's Bunch friends, asked me if she could print their pictures and give them to the kids. I said I can help you with that! I started brainstorming (you know by now that is my favorite thing 😊) and gave her the idea of doing signs and little cards with stamps. Each card had a special message, such as "I believe in you" and "you got this." She really likes them! I am now working on them so when she gets them, she can give little positive cards to the kids when they visit her office. They will at least have a little hope. A little love from their friends, the doggies of Prada's Bunch.

God loves in many ways. Doing this is a beautiful way to show his love.

Thank you, Carrie, for letting me help you with this project. I am truly blessed and honored. I will show you the final little cards when I finish!

I even have some in Spanish for her Hispanic kids. I love them all so much.

I gave one to my Cristy when she was about to start her new journey and she thought it was awesome!

Love to all, Silvia

The cards were wonderful gifts to the kids. One girl glued the picture to her ID card. She said that every time she felt sad, she would look at the picture of Prada with the sign "I Believe in You" and she would smile and move on.

I was in heaven! All these beautiful messages.

Other Prada's Bunch friends wanted to receive these cards for their kids. I absolutely loved the direction this journey was going.

After a few weeks, Carrie said that the kids have shown a big interest in Mami Prada and wanted to know more about her. I said, "Let's become Pen Pals!" And so, we did!

Carrie decided to work with a class, and there were six kids.

For the rest of the year, we were Pen Pal's friends. They first wrote to Prada. Beautiful drawings and words like "You are so beautiful Prada. I love You Prada!" It was so special. I created a package for each of them with a letter from Prada with her paw print as a signature and her picture. A shirt and many little gifts. One of the girls that had trouble at home, she said "I have a Mami that loves me, and that is Mami Prada." I cannot begin to tell you how moved I was when I read those words.

The kids absolutely loved the Mami Prada letter and all the gifts! We did that until Christmas break. After that, a few of the kids left for other schools and others moved. The ones that are still in the school would talk about her and remember Prada with so much love. I will forever be grateful for the opportunity to make a difference in their lives.

The little cards were loved by so many. I started to make bookmarks with the messages and pictures. We even had a series with Dr. Seuss quotes. Many friends that were teachers got them for their kids.

Our journey of love and adventure was getting interesting. I was finding ways to help others with my dogs' help, through my creativity and my hard work.

Our 2017 calendar was sold out. My promise was that every year, I would donate part of the proceeds to a rescue organization. I found two rescues that I wanted to help. One was here in Miami called Born Free Pet Shelter. We donated a portion of the proceeds when we went to visit the facility. Their manager Maria Elena was exceptional, and we also became incredibly good friends and through the years we donated to them on many occasions. They were a non-kill dog shelter and needed help in many ways.

In 2020 we donated more than $500 in items and food for the shelter. Maria Elena came to our home and personally got it all. She, Prada, and the kids had a beautiful photo together that truly showed gratitude and love.

An incredibly special golden retriever rescue called Joshua's House of Golden Retrievers in Tampa, Florida, was my other rescue. I contacted them and told them that I would like to make a special donation on behalf of the followers of my page Prada's Bunch who many were also followers of the rescue. They were incredibly grateful, and we agreed on a day for me to go by and take the donation in person.

On March 5, 2017, Miguel and I went to visit this amazing organization. We loved their home so much, their dogs and the special people that ran it. We were welcomed with open arms. It was truly special to see the love and dedication Miss Ellen and her husband provided for the dogs they rescued.

I posted this that day:

Mission Accomplished ♡🙏🐶

I cannot begin to describe how beautiful this place is. It was truly a blessing to meet Miss Ellen, Miss Sharon, and their husbands, and of course all the furry kids. We had a wonderful time under the trees while I told them about Prada's Bunch and Friends and all the awesome adventures we had. And of course, about how all of you helped us to achieve this goal. We are so proud to give them $1,000. A remarkably high goal that I set up when I made the calendar. They sure deserve the help! Franklin is doing great, and Murphy was able to walk after extensive surgery. Joshua is a darling boy. He runs and is a total joy on three legs. All of them were so loving and expressive. I got my huge share of kisses! This is a home. A beautiful home for dogs. A perfect sanctuary for goldens. We are blessed to have the chance to be here. Thank you, Miss Ellen, for lunch and for listening to

my endless talks about us and all our missions and adventures. We hope to help as much as we can and hope one day you can enjoy the Bunch. ♡

Our journey of love and adventure had many roads. Helping the kids to feel better, sharing our cards, bookmarks, signs of love and support. Not to mention the amazing deed that was helping organizations and different people that rescue dogs, which is special and an extremely difficult endeavor. I was glad that what we did, made other people happy and that our contributions made it possible for them to do a little extra.

I was convinced that God gave me the opportunity to make something that I never thought I was good enough or capable enough to do. I was an ordinary person following the mundane way of life. Work, kids, the house, etc. I was afraid I was living a life with no meaning or purpose. My kids grew up and became more independent, therefore, they did not need me as much as when they were little. I was not a doctor or a musician or a scholar or an amazing person that people thought could change the world with her presence or knowledge.

I was lacking meaning in my life and when I finally died people would say at my funeral "Oh she was a nice person, a great wife and a good mother, nothing extraordinary." It scared me, to be honest.

Then the decision to have Prada's puppies brought Prada's Bunch into my life and suddenly I felt alive. I brought to life a Facebook page with everything I had, my love, my creativity, my imagination, my kindness, and my hard work. Even through tough times and sorrow, I opened my home to strangers and gave them love and companionship, and a peek into my vulnerabilities and strengths. I took care of every aspect of my life and then some.

I was happy to do what I was doing. But there was something still missing. I wanted to make an everlasting difference. I wanted to find a more tangible way for me to pay back all the blessings that we have received.

I felt that just posting about our day was not good enough anymore. I needed to do something monumental.

Then a thought came into my mind. I have experienced how much love people have for my dogs through Prada's Bunch. Dogs are amazing to people. I had an extraordinary connection with them. What if I found a way to include them in my quest? What if I could find the perfect way to express what I feel? What if I can share with people in my community; people I can see in person? What if?

And that thought became a reality. It was the purpose I had looked for inside me all my life. The part of me that was waiting for the right time to surface. The part of me that was sure that I could make a difference. Not only that, but I could pay back the blessings we have received in so many ways. I could demonstrate that all is possible if someone has the will, the passion, and the love for it.

Our journey of love and adventure suddenly found a new road. I found it. No what ifs. But what is it? And how amazing could it be?

One night I sat back and realized that before Prada's cancer the thought crossed my mind. But I disregarded it. Little did I know that I had the vision and the plan. It was time to make it happen. I had butterflies in my stomach thinking what this would mean to me. I had no fear. No doubt. I felt peace.

This is what I love and can do and how special is it that the dogs that changed my life were part of it? I cannot wait to tell you about it!

Let's go kids, we got work to do.

Our Journey of Love and Adventure

Chapter 11

*"Everyone thinks they have the best dog.
And none of them are wrong."*
W.R. Purche

Love is a Four-Legged Word

How do you pay back kindheartedness? Blessings? Support? Unconditional love?

These questions were in my heart the minute that I started to receive the love and support from all our amazing friends. After a few brainstorming sessions and research, I found the best way to do it. My dogs and I have a new mission.

We were going to become therapy dog teams! YES! We were going to learn, train and become the most amazing teams ever.

Prada's Bunch Therapy Dog Teams! Sounds great, don't you think?

The day I was ready to announce it, I posted this:

Hi Friends!! I got news!!

I have been researching the best way to make a difference and pay back all the blessings we have received since the Bunch was born. We will start our therapy dog journey! I found out that the best way to go is to become a member of the organization Alliance of Therapy Dogs. They have a lot of information and guidance. I want to learn and really be prepared to do this right. They have great policies; they offer help, give lots of tips, and provide insurance as well. They require four observations to receive the certification. Charlie will be first to train and get certified. They want to make sure Charlie and I behave properly 😊😁🙂. I am extremely excited and nervous!! I cannot wait to tell you about it. Tomorrow at 1 pm we will have our first observation at an assistant living facility. Wish us luck!! 🤍🙏 I know God will guide us and the angels will make sure Charlie is in his best behavior!! Charlie will get his Canine Good Citizen Certificate as well. 🤍🤍🤍

Our friends were so excited for us! They believed in us and knew that we could make it happen. They support us all the way.

This new goal of mine was going to be executed in separate phases. And one dog at a time. The three of them were wonderful with people. But I always knew that Charlie had the most calm and sweet temperament. I chose him to start this journey because he was perfect for the job.

Our journey into this new adventure began with Charlie and me.

Our first observation was at The Palace, an assistant living facility. That was the most amazing experience! That day we learned so much. We met many new friends that were there for the same purpose. The observer gave us instructions and we got to go inside the facility and meet the residents. That day, March 25, 2017, was the date my grandmother passed away a few years before. It was bittersweet to see ladies that looked like my grandmother. I knew somehow someway she was guiding me through this special day.

We learned the basic ways to meet and greet the residents. What to do and how to do it. Making sure that Charlie was always safe and that we managed to navigate among furniture, wheelchairs, and other equipment.

We learned to greet those that were not able to physically interact with the dogs. How to guide their hand for a soft petting and respond to any of their requests. Then we met with the active youthful residents. All smiles and love they were. The dynamic was different but still we were to follow the same rules. At the end of the visit, we met with the observer to check mark our test papers. We got all good! Cheers for Charlie and me! We did good!

We were so excited and exhausted! I remember we got ice cream and celebrated together the beginning of a special journey of love and adventure with my partner in crime, Charlie Brown.

Between the observations we continued with training. Charlie was finishing the advanced classes and then he was going to have the test to be a Canine Good Citizen! That meant that he was qualified to be introduced to public places where he would be on his best behavior.

On March 27, 2017, we completed the first big step!

May I present you CHARLIE BROWN ♡🐾📷 CANINE GOOD CITIZEN ♡📷🐾 Woohoo! Charlie passed all 10 points on the test!! So proud of him!! And his friends Rufus and Rocko also passed and graduated from the advanced class!! Thank you for all your encouragement, love, and support!!

Cheers for Charlie were in order! Our friends were so excited and supportive.

I found out that close to our home was an assistant living facility called The Residence. I wanted to share a few calendars with them since I know they love to see pictures and remember their own dogs. What I did not know was that this was the opening door to our grand adventure!

We got our first job as a therapy dog team!

This was my post:

Good morning 🌼 we have awesome and blessed news!! ♡ 😊

Charlie got his first volunteer work!! ☆ Yesterday I took the calendars to the assistant living facility near our house. Well, God's

time indeed is perfect!!! 🙏 Alicia, the activities director welcomed me. I mentioned that I wanted to donate the calendars and share that we would soon become a therapy dog team. She could not believe I was there! She said she had been looking for pet therapy for a long time and was not able to get it! We both were so happy!!! She said, "this is a match in heaven." ♡😊🙏🧖

Charlie will start on Sunday, April 2. She was so excited when she saw the calendars! She could not wait to show the residents! I need to make a bio and send a picture of Charlie to her. She will make flyers to introduce Charlie!!! ♡⭐ this is SOOO exciting!!!! I hope and pray all goes well!!! It is really a dream come true. ♡ Thank you for joining us in this new journey of love!!! ♡

The visit was amazing! Charlie did so good and was gentle, calm, and loved all the residents. Our first day on the job was a total success! We recalled all we learned and what we were supposed to do. We were so new to this. We were grateful Alicia gave us the opportunity to practice while we got our certification. We just had to show proof of vaccination and a rabies tag.

During our training and learning our new job, I kept posting all the shenanigans of our lives.

Good morning, good night, and happy Friday! Those were my favorites. The kids were two years old, Mami Prada was seven years old and

Uncle Spiky was 12 years old. But all of them were full of mischief and silliness.

We had a new birthday post modality. I posted the backstage pictures and pretended they were talking to each other. It was hilarious! I was so proud of myself for producing these little sketches. It was truly so much fun.

We have a small boat. We live near the Florida Keys, and we love to go on boat rides. We took the dogs on the boat one day with their life jackets. Well, it was a messy mission to say the least. They swam and got sick too. They were definitely like a fish out of water. Miguel was not a happy boat captain, let me tell you.

Mami Prada was in heaven! She loved the wind on her face, diving in the water and swimming to catch the ball. We took tons of pictures and celebrated life!

But life also brought another very painful heartbreak. Late in 2016 my dad was diagnosed with pancreatic cancer. Those were exceedingly difficult months for me. It was so scary to think that I may lose one of the most important people in my life. My dad is an amazing man. I said is because by the grace of God he survived. It was a tough time for my family. He had very extensive surgery and then chemotherapy. He never let go of hope. Family and friends, all prayers warriors were there for him, He fought cancer with all his might.

My mom was always beside him and took care of him. Their commitment to love and to sickness for each other never faltered. I knew that their example was also a sign for me to keep fighting for what I wanted.

Life is too short. They taught me always to never miss the opportunity to make a difference. I wanted to make them proud of my determination to continue with my quest. And they loved every step of the way I took into

my new journey. Their support and encouragement were always with me.

Due to his fragile state Ruby came to stay with us for a few months. It was so special to have her home, but I knew she missed them, and they missed her.

We were so thankful when my dad finally completed his treatment and little by little got his strength back. We were so fortunate and grateful for his health. Ruby went back to their home, and it was the most amazing reunion ever. She was his guardian and never left his side. She knew he needed her love. Watching them interact made me realize that I was going in the right direction.

Love is a four-legged word.

Charlie and I continued our training. We went back to the assistant living facility for two more observations. The observer said that she was satisfied with our performance and there was no need for a fourth one!

We were ready to submit our paperwork to receive our certification.

Our post was this:

Personal Note:

Yesterday I took this envelope to the post office. I had so many emotions going on. It may seem silly for some, a simple task.

But to me, this is a dream. A goal. The beginning of a beautiful journey.

On this day, my dream became a reality.

I cannot tell you how proud I am of my determination and hard work. How blessed I am to have these kids that have shown such beautiful love to us and others. Charlie came to stay with us by chance. And I thank my lucky stars

that he did. I cannot wait to begin to train my sweet mami and our unique Lalique. Each has a mission. And I am determined to help them accomplish it.

Thank you. All of you. Your love, support, encouragement, and praise is fuel to my soul. To my will.

Love you all. I cannot wait to share with you all our journey!

Silvia.

On May 10, 2017, we received our certification. Charlie was officially a therapy dog. And I was his handler. I was bursting with pride. We did it!

We received a beautiful certificate with his name and mine. And it brought with it an incredibly special token. A red heart token that read: Registered Therapy Dog - ATD

I had tears in my eyes when I held this token in my hand. It meant so much. It meant Charlie was officially certified to make people happy.

I got him a beautiful red vest. It had a big patch in the middle that read: "I love working for hugs and kisses" on one side with his name "Charlie Brown Therapy Dog" embroidered and on the other side, it said "Prada's Bunch and Friends" with a heart with a paw print inside. It fit him like a glove. He was so happy and ran around the house wagging his tail. He knew this vest was his own "Armor of Love."

We got bandanas and a special bag to hold his goodies during visits. Treats, a ball, credentials, a water bowl, and poop bags. We set up a basket with brushes and perfume and wipes to make sure he was nice, clean, and super delicious for his visits.

Now we needed to find places to visit and make people happy!

Our journey was going to become an amazing experience. To be honest, I did not know the monumental task I was signing on for. But by God, I thought I was ready. But I also had some trepidation. I had moments when I felt a bit anxious and insecure. What if something went wrong? What if I did or said the wrong thing? I was going to do this on my own. Was I ready for this commitment?

Let's hope and pray.... And see... Our journey of love and adventure took a turn for the better.

Chapter 12

"The bond with a true dog is as lasting as the ties of this earth will ever be."
Konrad Lorenz

All For the Love of Dogs... and Humans

During my research to figure out what a therapy dog team does, I learned that the main venues for the therapy dogs to visit are hospitals, nursing homes, libraries, and schools.

I wanted to volunteer at all of them.

But there was a problem. I work full time for my dad's company, so my volunteer work had to have a very unusual schedule. We could only volunteer on weekends and after 6:00 pm on weekdays, with the occasional escapade on a weekday to visit a school.

It was time to call and figure out who wanted pet therapy at their facilities with a very unusual schedule. Lucky for me all of them did!

We already had the job at the assisted living facility close to home. But we needed to register as volunteers with other places too.

I contacted the volunteer department of a big hospital that was located right across the street from our home. West Kendall Baptist Hospital. I made an appointment and Charlie and I showed up. It was love at first sight! The volunteer coordinator, Miss Hovde, was delighted and said they would welcome therapy dogs any time, any day! She loved Charlie and after that we became amazing friends.

After the orientation and setting up the schedule we were ready to go. Every Tuesday night at 7:00 pm we were set to visit the patients and nursing stations, as well as the ER.

This was our first post for the hospital:

We had our first visit to West Kendall Baptist Hospital. What a blessing! ♡ 🐾 🏥 We met our new friends Miss Gabriela and her husband Carlos. They are also volunteers and will be helping us during our visits. They went into the patients' room before us and asked the patients if they wanted to meet Charlie and gave them Charlie's card. There were a few patients that did not want a visit from him, and that is ok. But we got to visit 20-25 rooms, nurse

stations and the front desk. We are not allowed to take pictures of patients, but I can assure you they all had at least three minutes of smiles and happy moments when they saw Charlie and got to pet him along with their family members. ♡🐶☺

You can see the nurses were head over heels for Charlie 😍 tons of pictures taken! And requests to come back from everyone! He behaved so well. Patient. Easy going, regardless of all the new smells and people. Even though it was a quiet time at the hospital, we spent

almost two hours. He earned his ice cream. 🍦♡ I am extremely grateful I got to work with Miss Cindy, the volunteer coordinator, Miss Gabriela, and her husband Carlos. They made this an incredibly special journey. We agreed that we would come back every Tuesday.

Thank you, friends, for your love and support and for believing in us. ♡🐶

After that day, we felt more confident in our work. Charlie was more at ease and trusting. He was learning when it was time to get ready.

We had a special routine when it was time to go on our visits. We had a table outside that became his "get ready" station. He loved it! I brushed him and got him all freshened up for the visits.

After each visit I made a post about it. I wanted to share what I was experiencing. Our friends loved and supported us every time.

Meanwhile the kids, Mami Prada and Uncle Spiky were having fun and doing all kinds of shenanigans. They had their weekly bathroom meeting that everyone loved. It was important for me to show our friends that we still enjoyed our time as family and that they also got their beloved posts.

Charlie and I registered in a click and trick class! It was so much fun! Charlie was learning tricks to show on his visits.

In one class he was learning to "read" SIT and DOWN. Our instructor gave us two big signs with the words. Well, a few days of practicing later at home this happened:

In Lalique's words:

Well mom. Let me tell you how it went.... Charlie said "Lalique! I need you to eat the signs!!! 🐶♂️ I really do not need to read, right?" I said, "Whatever you want dear brother!!" See. He is ok with that 😇 Hmm what

about dad's hat?? 💡 Ohh well. I could not resist for the life of me! 🐻 it smelled just like daddy 👶 and you know how much I love dad!! 👫

"Ohh little girl!! What am I going to do with you??" 🐱 my mom said. I told her, "Love me just like you do. Because you are my mom." 💝 And then I did my trademark head tilt and melted her heart.

Everyone adored Lalique and her mischief. They knew she was responsible but nevertheless they defended her. Her fan club was tight, and they would never let her take the blame. It was silly but oh so special. That simple post of a silly mishap brought so much joy to all.

Every day our friends expected a good morning.... And a good night.... If I did not post for one day, rest assured one of them would send a message. Is something wrong? Are the kids and Mami ok?

How special it is to be loved and cherished like that. We were and are blessed for all the love we received.

We still made our famous birthday posts for all our friends. We added balloons and other cool hats. It was special to receive a birthday request for Prada's Bunch. People shared it on their pages and shared with us how much they love it!

Mami Prada was feeling great, all her regular checkups were good and there was no evidence of anything amiss. Life was good for us.

Our quest to get new places to visit was in full force. I contacted the humane society. They had a division for therapy dog visits. I talked to the director, she was nice and after I shared my credentials made me part of her group. Through her I contacted Miami Dade County Public Library System. There was a library in my area that was really interested in having therapy dogs for their reading program.

I called the library and got an appointment to visit.

This was our post:

What a great visit we had at the library! Charlie was great ♡📚👍🐶 Miss Alice loved him and wanted to have us as a therapy dog reading team. We are going to go twice a month. On Thursday we will visit the other library that she also manages so we can participate in that one too. 👍📚🔍🐶 Unfortunately with technology kids are going to the library less and less. This may be an incentive to get the love for reading back in this amazing world full of knowledge. She said she is going to order a poster with Charlie's picture! 😎 and we are going to practice with some friends to make sure Charlie behaves properly👍. This is extremely exciting!!! ♡📚🐶 thank you for coming along in this new adventure!

We scored not one but two libraries! Miss Alice at the Concord library was really impressed that Charlie was bilingual. He understood English and Spanish. He was going to be a great asset for all patrons of the library.

Now, I have gotten myself in a big predicament. To be honest, I was not really prepared with this side of therapy dog work. My kids were 20 years old and 18 years old. I have not dealt with small kids in an exceedingly long time. I did not know how to make this library program work. Did I make a mistake committing to something I was not ready for?

What could I do?

Our Journey of Love and Adventure

By now you know me a little better. And you would think. You got this Silvia! I appreciate your vote of confidence. I really do. But I was in uncharted waters. I needed help! And fast!

Thankfully, Google was available to help ease my anxiety. I found a program that works with schools and libraries together with a therapy dog organization. This program is called R.E.A.D. Reading Education Assistance Dogs. Bingo!!! I found the solution to my problem!

I contacted one of their directors that happened to be in Tampa. She was having a workshop to teach therapy dog handlers how to work with kids in schools and libraries. That was a huge relief! Meanwhile, she sent me a few videos and materials for me to review. I learned the basics

and with that I felt a bit more prepared to face this new area of therapy dog volunteering. I drove all the way to Tampa for a weekend and got certified. Charlie was a R.E.A.D dog! How awesome! I learned the fundamentals and I added my own touch. We were ready.

My son Carlos had a friend that had a sister who was about 10 years old. I had an idea! I contacted his mom who was also my friend and I explained that I needed help. Charlie and I needed to practice our reading program with real kids. She was delighted and agreed to have Charlie and me over at her house. We loaded up the car with his blanket and a few books and off we went!

We had a little field trip to our dear friend Mayte's house! She and her daughter and friends were kind enough to help me and Charlie "practice" reading time. ♡📖🐶 Charlie needs to get used to relaxing and just laying down when the kids are reading. It is a little challenging. I reached out to my friend and headed over.

We used some treats to lure him to stay put lol!! After reading I took his vest off, and Charlie was free to play with the kids 🩷😊 I know it will take time and practice. We still have a few days before we go to the library! Any volunteers want to read with Charlie?? Thank you, my friend!!! Love you all! 🩷🐶😊

Our friends had such a positive attitude. They all encouraged us and told us not to worry! Everyone would love Charlie and he would do so well and be so happy to be surrounded by kids that would pet him.

Our page had about 2,700 followers! I was in awe! So many people looked at our adventures and all we did. It was an honor to bring love, laughter, and experiences to everyone.

Weekends, after our visit to the nursing home, were all about fun! And baths. They got to play in the pool. They loved swimming and retrieving all kinds of toys so much. Many pool toys were destroyed in the process. I discovered then that old sneakers were the best pool toys for retrievers. They had a blast! Mami Prada

especially. She loved water! She was a diver, and she would bring her shoe and place it on my feet and then she sat and looked at me and then the pool. Throw it, her eyes said! And I obliged. Her wishes were my command. It was a ritual. I was there to be their pool assistant. Lalique and Charlie used the pool stairs and swam across the pool to get the shoes Mami Prada left behind. And just like that we spent hours until it was time for a bath.

You may ask about Uncle Spiky... where was him during this pool party? Well, he was nowhere to be found! He did not like the pool or baths for that matter. It was a mission to find him when he got a hint that it was time for a bath. Our friends absolutely adored his grumpy faces after each bath. He was so loved. He was called "The Boss" and make no mistake, he really was.

We kept up with our visits to the hospital, the libraries and the assistant living facility. Our posts were getting better and better, full of anecdotes and me telling them how good Charlie behaved.

Charlie got a poster made by the hospital. It had his picture and said: "Welcome Charlie Brown, Today's Pet Therapy Dog" we put it up every time we visited. It was like a big "Hello Honey, I am home!"

I love to share the love for Charlie:

♡ 🐾 🏥 Charlie's visits are so special and rewarding. We saw about 25 patients and several nurses and staff. They were so happy to see Charlie. They took his picture, hugged him, pet him, and even some patients' family members went out of the room and followed us, so we did not miss visiting. 🐶 There were a few that even remember him from previous visits. It was the highlight of my day when my friend Gabriela went into the nurses' break room and told them Charlie was here... oh how they started screaming "OMG Charlie is here!" 😊 and when we went to visit the nurses in the ER, it was the same. Patients were trying to see what the ruckus was about. Such a blessing! All through it, Charlie was patiently smiling, sitting for pictures, and letting them have their fill in hugs and kisses. ♡ he is a master of snapchat selfies!

One of the librarians was talking to me about what I do with Charlie. She asked if I receive any compensation. I said yes. I receive the love, the blessings, and the happiness in my heart to see smiles, eyes light up and tender hugs to Charlie and I even get some too from young kids to the elderly.

"I am a little pencil in the hand of a writing God, who is sending a love letter to the world," as Mother Teresa said. I absolutely loved what I was doing and the places we visited. But there was one place that my heart was looking for.

I was really pushing myself. I worked full time, came home, got Charlie ready and went volunteering. We went to the hospital and the library at night during the weekdays. We went to the assistant living facilities and another library during the weekend. I took care of my home and my family. How could I add anything else?

But God had a plan, and I was doing his deed. I had another extra mission to complete. One that forever changed my life.

Chapter 13

*"The dog was created especially for children.
He is the god of frolic."*
Henry Ward Beecher

A Loving Paw for the Children

I watched videos about therapy dogs. I wanted to learn, and I wanted our work to be special. One of the videos showed therapy dogs visiting Children's Hospitals. I got a special tingling inside. I said to myself "This is your call. You can make a difference in these kids' lives."

Remember I said that I was not familiar with "how to be around kids" anymore or help them since mine were grown and my other kids were dogs? I changed that statement after I started volunteering with the kids at the library. I opened my heart, my mind and my attitude and learned all about sharing with kids.

Going to the library and reading with the kids helped me see them in another light. I learned so much from them. I spent time really looking into their eyes, sharing stories, talking about themselves and how they felt when they sat with Charlie on the carpet. Even with me. I got many hugs. I even got little tykes sitting on my lap for me to read to them.

They trusted me and I was so honored to receive their love. It was no longer a program. It was my sanctuary. Me and Charlie and the kids.

Charlie was so loving and kind to them. He let them pet him while they read, and he sometimes fell asleep. That was a sign that he trusted the kids. They wondered if he was paying attention! I told them that Charlie had a superpower: He could listen with his eyes closed. That got tons of giggles! When we were finished, he did tricks and the kids rewarded him with treats and laughs. It was an hour, and sometimes even more, of genuine love and special times.

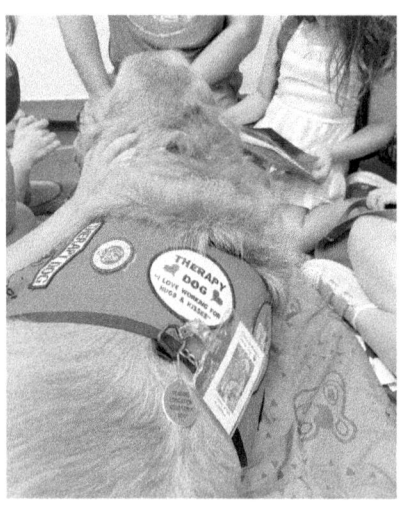

We even had the chance to meet kids from Prada's Bunch. Our friend Dania and her triplets came many times to enjoy reading with Charlie. It was special to see them and talk to them in real life. They even went to our house one time to meet Prada and Lalique.

We had a few kids with disabilities join us at the libraries. Some were loud and impulsive but gentle in their own ways. We loved to help kids with disabilities and let them enjoy a few minutes with us. With the guidance of their parents and me, we taught them how to be gentle with Charlie and how to approach him. It was truly special to see their faces light up after realizing the feeling they got when their hand touched the soft and light fur. Sometimes, we walked together a short distance with them holding part of Charlie's leash. They felt so happy to be walking beside Charlie. I even made a sensory shirt for Charlie. I placed items of different textures on the shirt and the kids played with them. They did not have the attention span to read a book or listen to it, so that is why I created a way for them to interact with Charlie without stressing them out. That was a good improvement to our activities.

We finally got to have the opportunity of my dreams during this special journey of love and adventure.

I was brave enough to contact Nicklaus Children's Hospital and applied as a pet therapy volunteer.

On June 2017 I posted this:

We got news!! 🐶 **I am so excited to tell you that we are in the process of finishing our volunteer application to visit Nicklaus Children's Hospital as a Therapy Dog Team** ♡🐶🐶 **we will keep you posted! I believe we will start July 11!** 🎊 **this is a wonderful opportunity and a dream come true for us!** ♡🙏

Our friends were so excited. They have seen our work and know how special our visits are. They were confident that we would be amazing at the children's hospital as well.

I did it! I took the leap of faith and committed to helping the children at the hospital. I was nervous, worried but so happy. It felt right. I was finally finding the place that would take my volunteering work with Charlie to a different level.

The application and orientation were time consuming and incredibly detailed. I had to apply as a regular volunteer and needed to know all the regulations and policies. That was okay with me. The more I learned the more I could help. I got my shirt the day I submitted my application. It was so special to see the light green shirt on my hand with the hospital logo. It was, in one way, my own "armor of love."

Meanwhile, life kept going. The human kids got into college. They started to work and find their own quests. I was there with them all the way too. My mission as a mom never faltered. They are my kids until God takes me to heaven. But I tell them not to be so relaxed when the day comes.

I will be watching them and annoying them all the same after life. They are amazing kids, and I cannot be prouder of who they are. They are kind humans that love and respect people. I am so lucky to have them. I love our family.

My dear Miguel understood my assignment. He knew how important it was for me to walk this journey. To do what I was doing. He learned to love animals and especially dogs when he met me. And he willingly accepted that. That is what love does to you. But I'm incredibly happy he did. He loves them and feels that my time sharing them with others is for a great cause. Not just for the people but for my own growth. We had late dinners and the once-a-month escapade to the Florida Keys to enjoy the boat. He helped me keep my mind clear and put my priorities in place. He seldom joked that I should find a hobby that pays. With all the time I dedicated to volunteering I would be a millionaire by now. I laughed and said, "Remember I get paid in blessings."

It was time to have a long break. I needed to have time for me and enjoy a few days off before I started my commitment at the children's hospital. I was tired and my body was letting me know. My soul also needed to be

restored and there was not a better place than my beloved cabin at the mountains of North Carolina.

It was the weekend of July 4. On July 1 we loaded the car with the dogs and off we went. We made it in about 14 hours this time. The dogs were bigger, and it was easier to go potty during the trip. We made it late at night, but we were happy and blessed to be in our happy place.

The mountain was beautiful! Full of green trees and rushing waters. The creeks were filled and so beautiful. Birds chirping in the morning and lots of wild animals walking through the woods. It was my heaven. I loved to sit on the porch drinking my coffee with the dogs by my side. This was what I needed to keep going.

We had so much fun and so many adventures! We walked the roads and played in the creek. Mami Prada was so happy showing the kids where to go and how to enjoy the creeks and ponds. Uncle Spiky was in his kingdom. He is

after all, the King of the Mountain. He never missed a step. He ran alongside the big dogs and kept an eye on all of them. He would bark at them when they went too far.

We posted every day about our adventures. The pictures and videos were amazing. They loved all of it. It made me so happy too that we were able to share our piece of heaven with the world.

We celebrated the Fourth of July with a wonderful picture with hats and red, white, and blue bandanas. And the beloved Flag of the United States of America. I have the most respect for this country and what it stands for. I am proud to be an American girl. And as Prada's Bunch we always celebrate the USA with love and reverence.

I had a moment to myself during this trip, impossible but true. The dogs were napping alongside Miguel. I was on my porch just sitting. Still. I remember I closed my eyes, took a deep breath, and started to think about my life. How I got to this point and if I was doing what I was meant to do. And I humbly said I was. Even through lots of sacrifices and countless hours of work I made a difference. I worked alongside my Charlie and showed strength and determination.

I cried too. Because I felt overwhelmed by everything I was living. The people I met at the hospital, their sickness and how difficult their life was going to be. The elderly at the nursing homes. Their fragile hands petting a dog that they do not recognize week after week. I wanted to hug them, and I did many times. I told them I loved them, and I meant that. Week after week we visited. Some we lost along the way. It is inevitable when you do this work, and you are caring and kind. It is hard not to

get attached. I wept for those beautiful souls that even though they would not remember, I made them smile. For the children that were afraid to raise their voices and read with confidence. For the ones who sometimes were frustrated and anxious. I cried for those that missed the love of a caring hand.

When I return home, I was going to be completely booked. I needed to also make myself aware of the monumental task I was getting myself into and how much work I was doing with Charlie.

I was afraid it was too much for him, too. How did he feel doing all this? I did not want him to feel that this was an obligation. Goldens are pleasers, and they would do everything they can to please you. But they do have limits and I knew that he was also affected by what we were going through. He was the leader of our team. People looked for him first and I did not want him to feel overwhelmed. I seriously considered that it was time for me to work with Mami Prada and Lalique to give relief to Charlie.

I am a very private person, unbelievably. I do not have many friends. I have dedicated my whole life to being with my family, my marriage, my kids, as well as Spiky and Prada. I have been working in the same company doing the same work for 30 years. Work that does not require interacting with outside people. I began to interact more with the world when Prada's Bunch was created, and I started volunteering with Charlie. I do not go out for girls' nights or even lunch with friends. I have Miguel, my kids, my family, and my dogs. They fulfill my life. Because of Prada's Bunch page, I have many special and wonderful virtual friends. That is the beauty of Facebook. It brought to life old friends and created new ones. And gave me the chance to make my life meaningful.

I took another big breath and told myself. You can do it because you have passion and a good heart. Keep working on your purpose and God will provide.

It was time to go home. We were rested and happy. We were ready to keep going and keep doing what we love.

I kept up with my fundraising efforts among my crazy and busy life. I made drawstring bags and totes. We sold out and the proceeds were collected and donated to Joshua's House. Our Prada's Bunch friends were happy to help and delighted to have something else that reminded them of our friendship.

Mami Prada and the kids were so happy to keep up with their shenanigans and receive love and encouragement from our friends. See, toilet paper destruction, pool parties, and snuggles were never in short supply.

Right before I was to start our visit to Nicklaus Children's Hospital, I was asked to shadow a team that was going to one of the areas of the hospital where the therapy dogs were needed. This area was the psychiatric ward of the hospital. I arrived at the hospital with my volunteer shirt on and my big smile. I was ready to meet the kids and learn from the team that was visiting that day. Since I was going to volunteer at night, this was the best place to go.

I met the team at the volunteering office, and we walked together towards the unit. I was a little confused when we did not walk right in. We had to call through the intercom and one of the nurses opened the door. She closed it and locked it right after we came in. I was not familiar with this and asked the volunteer why it was locked. He explained to me that here the kids are supervised by the nurses themselves. No parents or guardian allowed. They are there because of mental health issues and because they had experienced traumatic events in their lives. Many suffered depression, anxiety, bullying and some even had tried to commit suicide. I was in shock. I saw kids that could very well be my own kids.

They all sat in a living room area, and some were in hospital gowns while others were in their own clothes. Some even had their school uniform. I sat in a chair flabbergasted. Why am I here? Why are they asking me to come to this area? I was supposed to visit the kids in their room and let them pet Charlie and be happy. I was hurting for these kids. I wanted to talk to them and learn what happened. My maternal instinct was activated. Because of privacy law, volunteers are not allowed to talk about that. We were only allowed to be there, let the kids pet the dogs and answer any questions they asked. I was confused and sad. How would this work out?

Well, God is incredibly wise, and I later realized he brought me there for a reason. See, dogs have magical powers. They can break any barriers we humans have and, in this case, kids have. The first time Charlie and I came in I saw this place with trepidation, yes, but with a different understanding. I had discovered a new purpose. And I was going to do the best I could to help them.

The volunteer office assigned three teams to visit every Tuesday at 7:30 pm. We were one of the teams. We also had Clooney and her mom Pilar. Clooney and Charlie knew each other. They both did their observations at the same time and both graduated. It was great to see a familiar face. Pilar and I became good friends too. We also had Walter and his dad Paul. They were a seasoned team. They had volunteered for a few years and were super helpful to Pilar and me when we started learning the ropes.

We became the Three Amigos. And the hospital was happy that our team did such an excellent job. Every week we met different kids. We seldom had one that came back. The kids changed completely when they saw the dogs come in. We each sat in different corners, and they rotated visiting each dog. They laughed, some even cried. They felt unconditional love. They touched soft fur and even got a kiss from a well-meaning lick. For an hour they were free of their pain and anxiety. They felt pure love.

I had made cards similar to bookmarks and stickers with Charlie's picture and the phrase "You rock, my friend. Love, Charlie Brown." They cherished these cards and stickers and promised to keep them with them forever.

This was our first post:

Today, our mission took us to Nicklaus Children's Hospital. We met so many beautiful friends. They love to see us. Charlie was a total charmer. ♡☺ **we met a group of teenagers. The girls were SOOO in love with Charlie's hair lol, they said it was so soft!! And his curls!** ☺ **it was so dear to see. They asked me about him when he was a baby, so with permission of the supervisor, I showed them pictures of the puppies when they were babies and through their first year. Ohhh they were delighted** ☺♡ **they wanted to know about Lalique and her mischiefs. We were together with two other great therapy**

dogs. Walter is a veteran! I wished I had taken a picture of him! Next time. 😊 his dad said Charlie took all the girls lol and Clooney. We met before at The Palace. We both got certified at the same time.

He is a super cutie♡ after we were done, I needed to go to the bathroom. We walked the main hallway. Well. It took us at least 20 minutes to reach the bathroom. We were stopped every step along the way and Charlie got more hugs and kisses! I am so grateful for Charlie. Thanks to him, my dream has become a reality. God bless him. The sacrifice is worth it ♡

Our friends loved it! They were so proud of Charlie and the work he was doing. And I humbly admit of me too. They appreciated my efforts and my hard work. I was incredibly grateful for their kind words and encouragement.

A week later, Baptist Children's Hospital got word of my work at the West Kendall Hospital and ask us to visit them too.

They told me that they had a wing with children receiving cancer treatments and children in the ICU. They thought our presence would help. How could I say no?

We made a visit, got our credentials and schedule. We were to go on Wednesday nights at 7:00 pm.

Oh Boy! I had gotten myself in big trouble! That is one of my shortcomings. I cannot say no, especially if it is to something that I absolutely love.

I had weekly visits to three hospitals, two libraries, and two assisted living facilities.

It was time to call the calvary! Charlie and I needed help!

Chapter 14

*"Do not think that love in order to be genuine
has to be extraordinary.
What we need is to love without getting tired."*
Mother Teresa

Our Journey Continues With Meaningful Stops Along The Way

Charlie and I had a system. I came from work, got him ready and off we went to do our visits to the facility of the day. Life was in full force.

On August 1, 2017, we celebrated a huge milestone:

Thank God for all your blessings and for keeping Mami Prada Cancer Free♡🐶🙏 this month we celebrate one year since she was declared in remission. And we are so happy to say she is!! 💐♡👏👏👍🌸 thank you all for love and prayers, support and well wishes. We are so blessed to have you all!!

This post went viral. Hundreds of likes and so many comments. Our friends were happy and so grateful for this. We celebrated this amazing deed.

Charlie was doing so great and was the most incredible and talented therapy dog. He had this unique way of looking at people's eyes. With soulful eyes and gentle smile. He was ready every time I said, "Let's go Charlie!" And when he saw me take out his vest, bandana, collar, and leash, he knew. He would follow me wagging his tail to our grooming table and looked at me saying, "let's do this!"

One of the most time-consuming parts of therapy dog work is grooming. Yes. It is! Especially if you have a big dog with lots of fur. Charlie required a weekly bath and lots of grooming right before a visit.

Our friends enjoyed the entire process:

Good morning rainy and yucky outside so I got a warm and nice bath🛁 in the tub! Mom tricked me to get in with a ball☺ ha! I know better now! But it is ok! 👍 I feel clean and fresh for the

upcoming week's visits!! 😊 I cannot wait for my friends to smell me and say ohhh Charlie you smell SOOO good! I wish I had your hair! So Cute! 😊 You all have an awesome week friends!! See you later! Time to dry off and nap! 😴

I took pride in our appearance. We needed to look professional. Charlie got his special bandanas, and I had my volunteer uniform. We were class acts!

While Charlie and I did our job, I was also working with Lalique at her advance training classes. She did awesome! She loved to learn new commands and was very eager to please. Little by little she became a mature dog. Well. She did have a bit of a rebellious girl in her heart at moments. But that is what made her the best. Lalique or how we love to call her, Cookie, is unique. And we love her as she is.

Unfortunately, Mami Prada had a problem with her ear right before we were going to start her therapy dog classes. She had a hematoma and needed to have it drained. We went to see Dr. Vazquez and she helped Mami Prada feel better. A little block on our road, but we had it covered. Lots of love and tender care, she was good as new in no time.

I also created, designed, and processed the sales of our 2018 Calendar!

It was so beautiful. It had tons of pictures of the dogs and their memorable adventures. Each month we talked about the adventure that happened and all the shenanigans that came with it. Many of our friends purchased it and sent pictures of it when they got it. We donated the proceeds to Born Free pet shelter. We were so honored by the love and support.

Our visit to the libraries was a remarkable success. We got the kids returning and we even created a book club. There is one visit that I want to share that I know you will love:

Every visit to the library is such an amazing time. Today we met our friend Gaby and her mom Dunia. ♡🧒👩 as well as a very shy boy and two girls. The first thing the boy said was, "I do not know English." I said, "that is fine. Charlie is bilingual so you can read him in Spanish." He got a book in Spanish. One of the other two girls was also extremely shy and asked me to read the book for her. I did. After a round of each of them reading a book, the boy brought a book in English. I said OK, let's try. And guess what? He. Read. The. Book. And not only that. He read it by showing it to Charlie! His mom was mesmerized. He had been in school here from Cuba for only six months and has never read a book aloud. She could not wait to tell his teacher. ♡ He even had the initiative to get a book and ask if everyone could read a page. We did that. And when it was the shy little girl's turn who did not want to read at first, guess what? She did!!! Mind you, I helped her, but she was able to read the words ok. After she finished, we all clapped and congratulated her (I do that every time one of them reads.) We told her we are immensely proud! I gave them Charlie's stickers. Oh, what a wonderful experience. The girls were so kind and helped me fold the blanket! So cute! ♡ Gaby got a beautiful picture of her and Charlie and made him a hat ♡. They are BFF! We are in the process of organizing a book club! So exciting!! He did not want to go in the car of course. Puffing and pushing we made it. It was a full wonderful day!

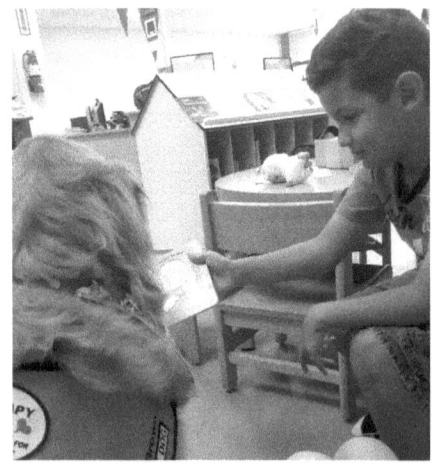

All our friends cheered and were so happy to hear the story! Felix came every Saturday and practiced his English by reading to Charlie. He won an award in school for "Most Improve ESOL reader." Mission accomplished!

About mid-September, Miami was hit by hurricane Irma. Work and visits were on hold, places closed, and everyone was on high alert.

We had to get ready to protect our homes and valuables. The hurricane was extremely strong, and our area was on its path. We brought home Miguel's parents since their home did not have hurricane shutters. Everyone worked all day picking up the yard and bringing everything inside. Dogs are extremely sensitive to storms. They knew and were restless. We tried our best to calm everyone.

My son Carlos was really concerned. He said "Mom we are not going to be able to find a shelter that will take us if something happens to our house! We are six people, four dogs, three birds and a turtle." Oh dear. He was right. We prayed we did not have to go.

Thankfully, we were safe and other than a lot of tree branches that had fallen, no major damage to our home or neighborhood. It was time to clean up and get back to life.

All our friends from near and far were sending messages asking us to please be careful! We are praying for you! We were so grateful. They were loyal friends. During the good and the bad, Prada's Bunch and Friends' followers never faltered.

As I get to know the people we visit, especially the nursing home across the street, I try to make our encounters a little bit special. I started to bring little gifts for them and for every major holiday I brought props and took their picture with Charlie. I loved to give them those pictures because I knew they cherished them.

Our last visit every week is to The Residence. ♡🐾🐶 we were so happy to see our friends!! We brought them flowers and took their

pictures which I printed and brought back to them. 🤍🐶😊🧒 they really like that. One lady said she has more pictures with Charlie than with her kids. 🤍 it is our absolute pleasure to help them feel special. 🐾 Charlie was so happy that our week is over that he had a happy roll in the grass! Lol (I am not sure why he did that 😝 silly boy). May God bless them.

Our friends posted feel good messages and were grateful we took the extra step to make them feel loved and cherished.

Another time I would go out of my way was when I met people at the hospital and they asked for a special visit in areas or rooms we would not normally go to. I confess that after an hour or so, Charlie and I were tired. But this time the effort was worth it.

Our post from our visit at the Baptist Children's Hospital was this:

It was a remarkably busy and eventful visit with Charlie and the kids at Baptist today 🤍 we got the surprise that Charlie's visit will be included in the pediatric ward bulletin board 🐶🤍👍 today we saw our sweet friend Valentina. She spent a good amount of time with Charlie and took pictures with him. God bless her 🙏🤍

There was a little kid in ICU of about three or four years old. He wanted a T-Rex dinosaur. Vanessa, our friend, made Charlie a dinosaur hat. 😊 Charlie looked SOOO adorable!!! The boy did not really care much. but he did say hi to Charlie. 😊 On our way to the ICU a mom asked me to visit her daughter. She really missed her dog. I said OK after we are done, we will visit. Their room was in

the new area of the hospital, so we had to cross the whole hospital to find their room. I promised I would go, and we did. She got SOOO happy! And Charlie got a good scratching on his chin and neck♡ 😊 finally time to go home. I needed a good pick me up, so we passed by Starbucks and Charlie got a well-deserved puppuccino♡ and mom a well-deserved caramel macchiato 😊

It was a great night for many. We are grateful we made them happy.

I have always kept track of all Prada's puppies. I get pictures and updates of their lives. Thankfully, they all were doing great. The one that I did not have frequent updates from was Mr. Blue. The original family decided to give him away because they had to travel a lot. To my surprise in October of 2017, I got a call about Mr. Blue. His name is Max. He was living with a family in a small apartment. Unfortunately, certain circumstances made them contact us. I was grateful they did. Here is the post about our Mr. Blue:

I promised them I would always protect them. Since the moment I saw them come into this world I loved them. I nurtured them and helped them the best I could, so they could grow strong and healthy. Today, each of them is a blessing to someone.

I promised them I would never give up on them. That I would always love them.

Today our dear Mr. Blue came back to our family. He was very loved and well taken care of by the family he was in, but circumstances made them make the hard decision to let him go. I went by to meet him again and he recognized me. He was all over me giving me "hugs" and kisses. We as a family talked, and my mom agreed to take him to her house. We talked to one of my sisters, and she agreed to take him. He will be my sister Luly and her kids' dog. He is incredibly special and sweet. Once he understood where he was and with whom he was, he relaxed and realized that he was safe. Which is an awesome development. He will be neutered on Friday and will receive training so he can be more confident and relaxed around other dogs and humans. I cannot wait for him to be reunited with the rest of the Bunch. He is now living with Ruby.

Welcome home Mr. Blue!

Our friends were understanding and sweet. They all wished him well. Max is living with my sister Luly and became her service dog. He is amazing. He loves his brothers and sister and the cats and is incredibly special to her. I am glad we got him back and that his life is now full of love and understanding. My sister brought out the best of him. She gave him a second chance. He was also becoming a great companion to her. They were there for each other for all the good and all the difficult moments in life.

We were blessed to have the opportunity to get together occasionally for our family group pictures. Max was still a bit unsettled and was not able to come to our Halloween photoshoot but later he was happy to participate.

I was also the dog costume designer and maker for family pictures. In 2017, Halloween pictures were extra special. Every night I worked on their costumes. I do not know how to use a sewing machine, but I am good with a glue gun. We decided to dress them all in Disney princess costumes. With Charlie being a prince, of course. Uncle Spiky had an incredibly special costume too.

Mami Prada was Snow White and Uncle Spiky the Grumpy dwarf. Lalique was Belle and Charlie the Beast. Lily Chanel was Sleeping Beauty and Ruby was Cinderella. Lulu, Lily Chanel's mom brought the Backdrop of Disney's castle and the wood floor. It looked so professional! And it was absolute mayhem! We set up the backdrop in our living room. After they played and were a bit calmer, we dressed them up. I made the costumes quite simple and easy to put on, so they did not feel uncomfortable. They knew what to do and did not disappoint. We only needed one exceptional group picture! Click! We got it! And then one of each. Mami Prada was so beautiful in her Snow-White gown. She truly enchanted our friends. It is by far my most favorite picture of all. After the photoshoot they got delicious treats for their amazing behavior.

♡🎃👻HAPPY HALLOWEEN! 👻♡🎃From Prada's Bunch Magical Castle♡

Mami Prada is Snow White 🐼

Spiky is Grumpy!

Charlie and Lalique Are the Beauty and The Beast 🤍🖤

Ruby is Cinderella 🩶

Lily Chanel is Sleeping Beauty 🖤

Thanks, Lulu, for bringing to life our beautiful Bunch through your lenses! 🤍

The post got tons of likes and so many loving comments. They enjoyed our family pictures and our shenanigans. What is not to love? Five golden retrievers and a Shih Tzu dressed like magic!

After Halloween, we settle back to our routine. Busy with the visits, packing and mailing the calendars, attending my day job, my house chores and annoying my human kids. It was no wonder I sometimes collapsed on the sofa some nights. But I was happy because I was doing what I loved. What is that Confucius saying… *"Choose a job you love, and you will never have to work a day in your life."*

Unfortunately, I had to work on my day job to pay for all the expenses of my Dream Job that paid in blessings. Oh well…. Life is funny sometimes…

It was time to reconsider my choices. I even thought of quitting some of the visits. I was worried about Charlie. It was a very hectic schedule.

But then I thought about the disappointment I was going to feel if I did that. I knew what I was getting into. But now, I had my doubts. It was time to act and find alternatives that did not involve quitting.

We needed Mami Prada and Lalique. I knew that they would be amazing. But I also needed the time to train and get them certified. I was confident now of what to do since I had a lot of experience with Charlie.

There was no time to wait. Let us begin....

Our new journey with the girls would be so special. I could not wait to see them in action.

Chapter 15

"Dogs do speak but only to those who know how to listen."
Orhan Pamuk

Mami Prada and her Magnificent Self

Mami Prada had already finished her advanced training before the kids were born. She was so smart and knew all the commands so well. I learned that Pet Smart opened a class specially for therapy dogs. Wonderful! That was the class Mami Prada needed to get ready for the observations.

It was a refreshment of the advanced classes with a little more in regards of equipment and situations that therapy dogs encounter during visits. It was taught by the same trainer that she had when she was a puppy. He was so happy and told everyone he knew Prada since she was a puppy and that she was the best!

Since I was already doing therapy dog work, I was able to help guide the new teams that wanted to get involved in this line of volunteer work. I was incredibly happy to share my experience and knowledge.

On November 4, 2017, Mami Prada started her observations at the assistant living facility where Charlie did his observations with Alliance of Therapy Dogs. We met the new observer and a few new friends. I was so proud to post this that day:

♡🐶 **She was born to be a therapy dog. I always knew that, but today she showed me how wonderful she is. It was like she had been doing it for a long time. She was never afraid of wheelchairs,**

walkers, or people. She went and said hi to every single person I took her to. And she was perfect when greeting her new dog friends. She really likes to lick, so I was worried about that. Even though she did lick a few hands, she was not excessive or bothersome. They just laughed and said she was sweet. Her first observation passed with excellence! ♡🐶🙏👍 Charlie is his mom's son. But each is unique in their own ways. So proud of both!

I was so happy! Our friends cheered for Mami and sent congratulations and encouragement words. They were looking forward to reading about Mami's visits. But first we needed to finish her therapy dog classes and observations.

On November 11, 2017, Mami Prada graduated from her therapy dog classes. I felt so proud of her. She was truly the best of the group!

Now, we needed to complete two more observations and mail our application. I wanted time to fly! I was looking forward to seeing Mami Prada in action.

Thanksgiving came around and we had so many blessings to be thankful for. The most important one was health. Our family, Mami Prada and the kids. We were all healthy and together. We made a special post to give thanks to all our friends:

Good morning 🍁 ☀️

It is Thanksgiving Week!! 🍁 **We want to express our gratitude for all our blessings, starting with YOU!** ♥ **We are thankful to have this wonderful family at Prada's Bunch and Friends where we share with you all our wonderful adventures.** 🐶**We are so thankful for all the love and support you give us every day!** ♥ 🍁🐾🐾🐾🐾**feel free to add in the comments why you are thankful this season.** 🍁 **have a wonderful week!**

We received many beautiful messages from our friends. It was rewarding to see their appreciation.

The Bunch continued with their shenanigans, and Charlie and I continued with our visits. Every week we brought love and happiness to the hospitals, libraries and to our friends who are young at heart.

It was time to celebrate Christmas and Lalique had a parade of hats to show to our friends. She loved hats and was always posing funny. It gave me lots of opportunities to make posts that made many people smile.

On December 15, 2017, we woke up to the news that we made it to 3,000 followers! How amazing was that!

Good morning ☀️🦁

We are SOOO excited here at Prada's Bunch home!! ❤️✌️We reached a milestone that we never thought was possible since we started almost three years ago. We were blessed to have the chance to open a page to share the puppies' adventures. The first week we reached 🎊500🎊 friends and Charlie was so happy to thank them! And today he and the Bunch did it again! We celebrate 🎊3,000🎊 every 100 friends we get; we post our journey beginnings so that many of you understand what we are all about. ❤️We have shared so much love and incredible moments. Some sad, some happy and all amazing! 🙏❤️thanks for all your love, likes and comments that keep us doing our best! We all have a purpose in life. And I am glad we can bring through the screen love, friendship, and laughter when it is needed the most. ❤️🙏

We love you all and wish you many blessings!

Welcome to all our new friends! And thanks to all who have been with us since the puppies were born January 1, 2015! ❤️👁️👍🙏 We love you!

It was truly special. I was surprised and grateful. We are accomplishing our purpose through the screen and in real life.

Because I am always looking for ways to help, I added Christmas ornaments to our fundraising efforts again. I made wooden frames with their Christmas pictures. Many friends got them and displayed the ornament with love in their own Christmas trees. Proceeds were added to the calendar donations for our shelters.

Many times, I also used my page to speak my mind and explain what is in my heart. I wanted our friends to also see what I saw and how I felt:

Personal note:

This is the dictionary definition of a therapy dog:

"A therapy dog is a dog that might be trained to provide affection, comfort and love to people in hospitals, retirement homes, nursing homes, schools, hospices, disaster areas, and to people with anxiety disorders or autism."

I cannot help but totally disagree with this statement.

You can train a dog to sit, lay down, stay, wait and so many other commands and tricks. But you cannot train to feel affection or to have that intuition to know when someone needs them. It is the extra sense they have that makes them get closer. To give their paw in a way that makes them feel connected with the human being they are trying to help. To know when to be quiet and accept the petting, the hug, the tender kiss on the head. To place their head in someone's lap and give them a lick on their face small enough to make them giggle. To allow humans in their personal space. You cannot train a dog to feel. The dog must have it inside their soul.

And that definition should also say a therapy dog needs to come with a patient handler. Someone that is willing to sit patiently while the dog works his magic and be aware of the dog's behavior, to be his best advocate.

I am humble to say that this is the most amazing experience I have lived besides being a mom. This takes my emotions to a whole different level. To be a therapy dog handler, as they call it, is not just to sit there and wait. You see the kids or adults experiencing what you love every day at home. It is to see that with every pet, every caress of their hands to the dogs' head or back or paws, you witness their emotions. They release their happiness, their sorrow, their pain, their hope. You chat and talk about your dog and laugh with them even though you wish you could hug and cry and hold them.

I encounter many people who tell me, "Oh I want my dog to be a therapy dog." And I will explain the basics. But really to be a therapy dog team, you need to give so much more than a nice dog and your time.

Today was an extremely grueling day. I cannot explain much. But I was glad I had the chance to give a kid and his brother a few minutes with Charlie and let them have the time to enjoy his company even though we were done and ready to head out. His dad asked with so much love and need. I just could not say no. It was like I was giving them a special gift. They petted Charlie, hugged him, and took pictures. They smiled, despite their situation.

I did cry after I left because I felt the pain and need.... and I could not do much more but give them what I could.

Please, if you ever consider being a therapy dog team, remember that it is a gift of love to others. Do it with love and respect and always find the blessings that come with every place you visit. Every person you encounter.

Thank you, friends, for letting me share this amazing experience with you. ♡🐶

Many friends commented with their appreciation and some that were also doing this line of work totally agreed with me.

One of our friends posted this quote: *"The meaning of life is to find your gift. The purpose of life is to give it away,"* Pablo Picasso.

Thank you, Picasso, your words are true and full of meaning.

I was indeed giving away my gift.

Finally, we were ready for Mami Prada's last observation on December 16, 2017!

May I present to you Mami Prada Therapy Dog ♡👍☺♡🐶 She did amazing! Sweet and very receptive to all the people at The Palace. She even got on the sofa to let the lady pet her. Mami decided she was safe enough to sit next to Miss Teresita, our observer, on the sofa and make sure she checked all the right boxes! ♡☺ So proud of mami and the next chapter in her journey! Now to send the documents and wait for her certificate😍 Thanks Friends for coming with us this amazing day!

Ahhh, we were all so excited! The likes and comments went off the chart! Mami Prada was on her way to making people happy in real life too.

I got her therapy dog vest, a new collar with her name and leash too. Her beautiful bandanas and bows. She was going to be the most precious therapy dog girl ever!

Christmas break was approaching and after all our visits were done it was time to rest and enjoy Christmas with the family! Their birthday was coming up! I could not believe the kids were going to be three years old on January 1, 2018!

We got mail! A wonderful box from our friend Mona from the Northwest Territories in Canada, one from Miss Colette from Massachusetts, one from our sweet friend Corine from Belgium and Miss Amy from Chicago sent gifts too. We loved all the gifts and delicious treats. So thankful for their generosity and friendship.

We went on a New Year's cruise with our whole family to celebrate my parents 50th wedding anniversary. That trip was special. We celebrated their life and love for each other. Even though I was having fun, I missed my dogs. I was looking forward to returning to their silly smiles and wonderful cuddles.

When we came back the dogs were so happy, and we were looking forward to celebrating their birthday.

Cristina, my daughter, woke up one morning with a very acute pain in her stomach and I had to rush her to the hospital. I was really scared. We did not know what was going on. She stayed in the hospital for a week. Finally, the doctors figured out it was her appendices. She had surgery and thankfully was okay. Since it was the hospital I volunteered for, I came one night with Charlie to visit her. She was so happy, and the nurses loved it too. We had a few stops by the room to say hello and wish Cristina good health. The funny part was that many did not recognize me when I was there, but they did remember Charlie.

When I met the surgeon, I knew I had seen her before. I remembered that I had a picture of her and Charlie. What a blessing. She took such diligent care of Cristina and told me how grateful she was to know us and the amazing work we do. Her surgeon cap had dogs.

We brought Cristina home and the kids and Mami Prada were so worried. They stayed with Cristina in her room giving lots of love and support.

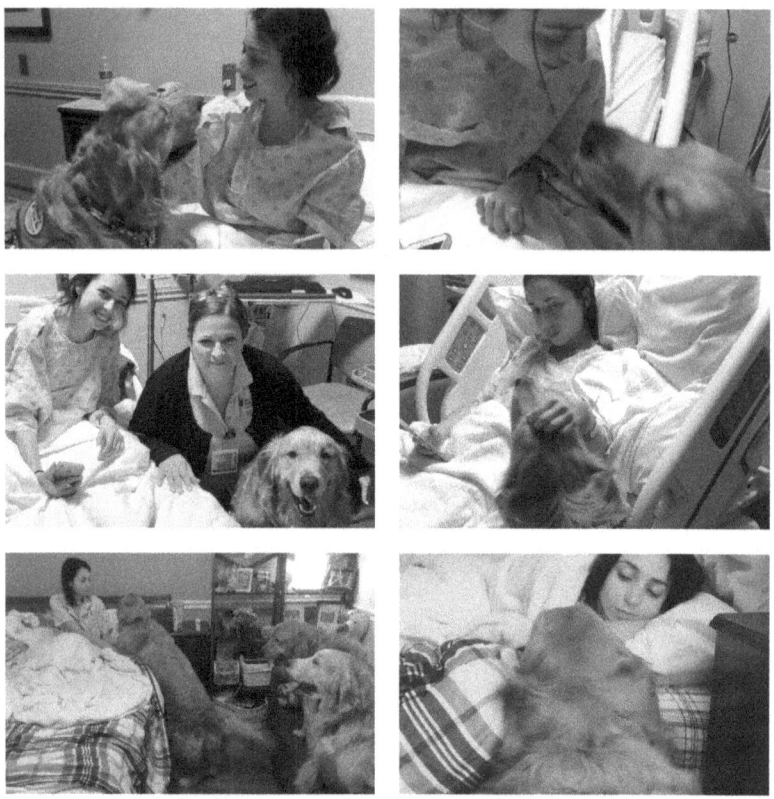

We were due to visit the nursing home by our house. I baked a sugar free angel cake and the residents gathered to wish Charlie a happy birthday! It was so sweet to see them all so happy and singing the song to him. He wore his birthday hat and ate cake with them.

We got a call that Lily Chanel's mom has had a bad accident. We went to get Lily Chanel and she came to stay with us for a few days. We were so worried about Lulu. But thankfully she was on the mend and soon would be home. Lalique and Lily had a wonderful time together! They took pictures with Lali's hat collection.

Spiky's birthday was January 19. We celebrated the kids' birthday and Spiky's. Mami Prada, Lily Chanel, Ruby, Charlie and Lalique sat on chairs around the table with their birthday hats and Spiky right in the middle of it with his delicious vanilla cake. They knew how to party! It was a wonderful day! After all the difficult days we encountered, it was great to have something to celebrate.

Charlie and I continued with our visits to the hospitals, libraries, and nursing homes. Each visit was special. We made tons of friends and kept spreading love and companionship.

On February 13, 2018, we got a special envelope.

It was a Mami Prada certificate and her red heart! She was official. Mami Prada and I were a therapy dog team!

It is with pleasure I present to you officially.... Mami Prada as Prada the Therapy Dog ♡🐶🐾🐕♡ I am so proud and happy to have my beautiful girl ready to bring so much hope, love, and joy to many. May God bless her and protect her in her new journey. I will send her certificate to the places where we volunteer and request to see if

I can alternate her and Charlie's visits. This will also give Charlie a break. I cannot wait to continue our journey of love and adventure. 🐾Next is Lalique! Hopefully, we can work on her super walk lol. Thanks so much for coming along in our journey and being part of it with love and encouragement. ♡🙏🐶🎀♀

Our post once again went viral. The love for Mami Prada and her news was exceptional. So many cheers, kind words wishing us luck and a blessed journey.

I added the symbol of "breast cancer survivor" to her vest. A reminder of the struggle and redemption. She was going to show the world that she was a survivor and a fighter. She was ready.

Mami Prada had an interview at the West Kendall Baptist Hospital. She was hired on the spot! That very same day we returned to the hospital at night to have her first visit.

♡🐶🏥Mami Prada had her first visit today at West Kendall Baptist Hospital. She was excited and so happy to meet everyone. Some realized she was not Charlie, and some did not. She won everyone's hearts. Charlie is special to many in this hospital. And I am sure Prada will also gain her place of love among them. They both are incredibly special and with different temperaments, but both are very well behaved and respectful, which I am so proud of.

I did feel a little bad for Charlie. He was expecting me to get him ready to go and I got a very pitiful look when I was leaving with Prada. I know it is silly, but it is a special connection we all have, and I do know they have special feelings for certain activities.

Mami showed how darling she will be doing these visits.

I will see how she does in the other hospitals. And I think I will assign them various places depending on their reactions. For sure Charlie is the best for the library since he is calmer for the kids. We will see. I am so blessed to have the chance to do this.

Now we need to work on Miss Lalique and see if she can handle this mission. ♡✌️👧 it was a wonderful first visit for mami.

The cheers and love and good luck wishes were so special. We had an army of angels wishing us the best of luck!

Meanwhile, Charlie took a week off to let Prada do training.

Good morning ☀️♡⛵

Well, since Mami is in training this week and I am home, I decided to take a little vacation! ♡⛵ Dad's boat is ready! I was just waiting for my brother Carlos to come over! Where is this boy! ok friends! Happy Wednesday! BTW I am immensely proud of mami! I know she is super good. I am just a tiny bit jealous she goes with mom instead of me. But it is ok. She needs to learn her ways. Oh, but I know I am the favorite boy of all the places we go😎♡

Everyone was happy he got a little break. He sure deserved it!

The next day we went to visit Nicklaus Children's Hospital. The whole volunteer department was in love with her soft eyes and beautiful smile. Again, she was hired. No questions asked!

Mami Prada rocked her second day at her new job! ♡🐶🌰✌️❉ **She got to the volunteer office and got in like she had been there several times. And what did she do? She got on the chair and got ready to say hello to the girls in the office. Yep. Just like the queen 👸 she is! She even got her picture taken for her badge ✌️.**

At Nicklaus Children's we only go to the special ward for kids with depression and other struggles with mental health. Today a special mission was given to us. Clooney and Prada went separately to visit one special patient who really needed some doggie love. We took a detour to meet this special girl. Prada walked in the room with the confidence of a very seasoned therapy dog 😊 since the girl was laying down and could not lift her head, Prada got in the chair and said hello. She spent a while there just sitting and letting the girl pet her. I was so pleased with her first experience with a person in a hospital bed. After the visit we came back to our assigned area. And yep. 😊you got it! She got in the chair and let the kids hug her and kiss her to their heart content. She then got down and rested for a few minutes until it was time to go. On the way she met volunteers and other staff members that melted when they saw her. ♡🐶

She is a natural at this even with all the excitement of the new place with so many people and smells. She inspires me to be a better person. 🤍🐶✌️

PS:

(Charlie is very much loved at the hospital and was missed today. He also gave me a little tantrum because I was not taking him. He got out of the door and sat right outside and would not come in. I had to do some convincing to get him back in the house. I wish I could bring both. Oh boy. I am in trouble now!)

"Aweee she is the best!" "You did great, Mami!" "I am so proud of you!" "Well done, Mami!" Tons of amazing comments and love for Mami Prada. It was truly dear to see how much everyone loved how well Prada was doing.

Next stop was the Baptist Children's Hospital. I sent her credentials in the morning and the volunteer office called to tell me that Prada was good to go! She could use the same badge she had from West Kendall.

Here we go! That visit went like this:

Welcome Mami Prada to Baptist Children's Hospital! 🤍

It is incredibly special to describe how Mami Prada did today. She was simply splendid🤍 Like she has been doing this her whole life. She came in with a bow on her head, a spring in her paws 🐕 and a smile in her face. She sat in chairs next to the beds and placed her paws on the side of the beds for the kids to reach her better. And in

one room, she decided she was there to stay with the girl and very discreetly jumped into bed. She brought a ray of sunshine with her! 🐶 laughter and big smiles since she was also going after the trays of food. There was a little kid laying sideways in the bed with his dad. He came in after a procedure and was very anxious. The dad was trying to calm him down. There were two poles of machines next to the bed and cables. We cleared a little open space so the kid could see Prada. Well, she moved forward disregarding the machines and cables and placed her face in the bed right in front of the kid. He petted her and calmed down. He gave her a cookie. He even said bye Prada when we were leaving. ♡

I am also in a discovery mode. They are both so different. While Charlie comes in with his suave swagger, mami Prada comes in with excitement. Charlie brings peace and calmness and smiles of content, mami is a little ball of happy fur walking in.

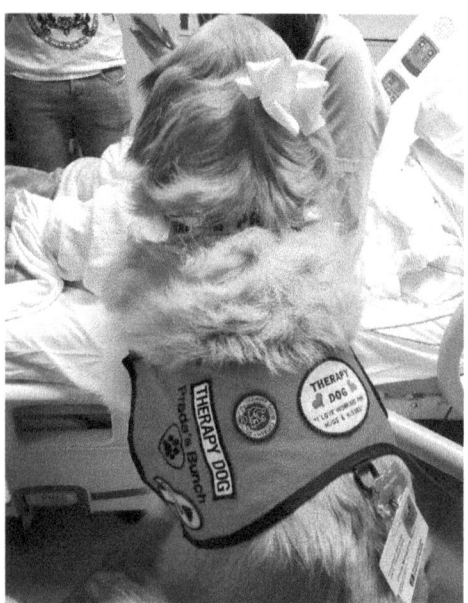

Both are delicate and special to the people and bring love and joy to those who meet them on their journey.

And for me, I learn to watch and appreciate the blessings and do my best to complement their amazing work. ♡🐕🐕🐾🐾 we are Prada's Bunch therapy dog teams. Living a journey of love and adventure.

Thank you for coming along with us ♡

Our friends were so happy. They knew Prada was going to be appreciated not only for her beautiful smile and softness but for her own personal journey with cancer. People saw her breast cancer patch and asked. When I explained they felt emotional and grateful.

I was in heaven! How amazing Mami Prada was! She was guided by an angel. I had no doubts. How sweet and tender she was with everyone. I could not believe my eyes.

Next day was Library Day!

Last year, Prada's superhero name was Super Kissy Woman. 😀 yep. There is a reason for that. She loveeeeesss to give kisses. And when you are in the library, you cannot do that. ♡ bless her heart! It was a super fun night! We made new friends, and our little girlfriends came again! We read a few books while trying to keep mami in place and not licking the kids' faces silly or the books 😊 We will leave this job to Charlie. 😉👋🙂♡ The kids were awesome and since they all love dogs and mami Prada, everything went well. 😄 Mami is such a charmer no matter what she does, everyone loves her!

I laughed so hard! She was truly a lover! She had no remorse. She was giving kisses and love to everyone that came close to her. I think we will leave the library for Charlie. It is safer for the kids.

I was so relieved. I knew my decision to bring Prada to volunteer with me was the right one. She surpassed all my expectations. I was also relieved because I was giving Charlie a break and Prada a purpose. We all need that little chance to demonstrate our capacity.

On February 21, 2018, we were contacted by ATD our therapy dog organization to see if we were available to help the Parkland Community after the horrendous event they suffered. Of course, we would! I contacted the person in charge, and we decided to go on Sunday to an event with many other therapy dogs that would come to help as well. Usually for these types of events, the therapy dogs that come are trained in crisis management with their handlers. I thought we could handle it and we went.

I decided to participate with Charlie. He is calmer, used to crowds and will know how to approach people.

Our friends sent a lot of prayers for strength and courage. It was a hard place to be.

We started the day at the event where we shared a couple of hours with lots of therapy dogs and people who came to provide relief to the community. But the real work for Charlie and other therapy dogs was when we went to the school. I am having a tough time trying to explain my feelings. All I can tell you is that this was one of the places that was extremely hard to be at. We came to the corner of the school where thousands of flowers, memorials, gifts and so much more were lying on the floor as a tribute of the love and sorrow for all 17 victims of the tragedy. As soon as we got there, we were interviewed by a news channel that was interested in our work (I will share it when I see it) then the work began. We stood for three hours in that corner, giving the children the chance to receive some love from Charlie and his friend Sophie. He met hundreds of hands that petted him and some hugs and kisses. We received so many "thank yous" for coming. For doing this. For helping. It was very humbling. The smiles we got when they asked his name were priceless and I gave away probably a hundred stickers which were received with a big smile and some even put them in their shirt. Charlie and Sophie worked side by side the whole time. What a wonderful opportunity to unite efforts. I really am blessed we became friends with Sophie's

parents. I am grateful for their hospitality since I live so far away and did not have a place to go between events. They very generously invited us over to their home to rest for a bit out of the sun before we got ready to go back to the school after the first event.

It is extremely hard to describe the feelings you get when you go there. It was a sober silence. You can feel the sorrow. As a mom, it really breaks my heart. I can only do what I can to help. And pray for those who lost someone.

There was a guy crying close by us. Charlie just walked away from me and stood close to his leg. It was very impressive to see his "I know he needs me" move.

I will, and I say it with my heart in my hand, come back any time I can if they need us. The power of love is strong. May God bless them all.

Thanks for coming with us on this journey. ♥🐕🙏

This post got lots of love, likes, and shares. They were grateful we went and offered comfort. They understood my feelings and prayed for me. I was very appreciative of their words.

The next day I woke up sick. My body was feverish and fatigued. I was very affected by this experience; it really got my heart and body. After a day or two, I was okay and ready to keep up with my hectic life. I did not have the luxury of too much time off.

Now it was time to get Lalique ready. Was she up to the challenge? We will see. She is a little different than the others and with a bit of apprehension about the outside world. But if we do not try, we do not know.... Let's give Lalique a chance to be the fourth member of our team. And conquer the hearts of all who meet her.

Chapter 16

'In times of joy, all of us wished we possessed a tail we could wag."
W.H. Auden

And With Lalique We Are a Team of Four

Since she was a puppy, Lalique was the troublemaker.

She handled many of the shenanigans and mischiefs. She had this way of looking so innocent and many times she got Charlie in trouble.

She has been a blessing to us in so many ways. The one that makes us laugh with her head tilt and her love for hats and the pool. I was not sure therapy dog work was for her. She was impatient, walked fast and got a little nervous when she was out of the house. But I did not want to hold her back and somehow, I knew I was going to feel terrible if indeed she was destined to be one.

I started to work with her while I was doing the visits with Charlie and Prada. We worked on walking and socializing at Home Depot. She genuinely wanted to do her best. She loves people! She was a bit guarded around other dogs which made me a bit uneasy.

We work together during her advanced classes, and she improved so much. She perfected her commands and was enthusiastic to do what was asked of her. On April 15, 2018, Lalique graduated and got her Canine Good Citizen certification. Our trainer was so proud. He worked with the three of them and all did amazing things!

I have the pleasure of presenting you with Lalique Margarita Mesa! 🐾🐕👏🧒🎓 Advanced Class Graduate and CGC certified. ✌️🐕🎉 She did amazing! I am immensely proud! She got two toys as a reward! ✌️🧒❓🐕 we did it!!! We are ready to start her journey to become therapy dog 🤍🐕👏🙏

The post went viral! Her fan club cheered for her, sent lots of love and congratulated us on a job well done!

Now it is time to schedule her therapy dog observations.

While we got that scheduled, I kept working with Charlie and Mami Prada doing our visits. We got invited to schools to be a special guest for Career Day, we visited the University of Miami library, Coral Gables library, and we became volunteers of Opuscare, an organization that offers hospice at nursing homes.

Mami Prada is really a joy to work with. She had already mastered the job of making people happy. ♡🐾🙌🖼️👧 We visited The Palace as Opuscare volunteers. We saw a gentleman that was withdrawn and since he was not looking at her, she went up to the chair next to him and looked at him. She got a little closer, so he decided to pet her. She sat there letting him pet her and even gave him a kiss. Then he smiled. ♡ and after that she went on. Sofas and chairs. She made sure everyone had a chance to be happy while she was saying hello. Some even got closer to say hi while she was with others. It was so sweet when she sat next to a beautiful lady in a wheelchair and just had a moment with her. It was a wonderful afternoon doing what she likes the most. Making others smile at her antics and kisses. ♡🙏🖼️👧🐾

Life was busy, but I kept up with it all. Sometimes I wondered why I got myself into these predicaments but then I remembered that once I was lost and without a purpose and I was not happy. I was now tired but happy.

As Picasso said, I was giving my gift away.

Our daily posts were a combination of good morning posts with mischiefs and our daily visits to the assigned facility, and always, our faithful good night post.

I think posting about the visits gave me a way to settle my heart. To process the emotions experienced during the visits. Some were extremely hard on me. Especially at the Baptist Children's Hospital where we visit the kids having cancer treatments.

She just lay down next to the girl and closed her eyes... If I knew better, I would say she prayed for her.

Some people would ask me how I did it. How can I spend time with kids that were sick? One would be surprised how resilient the kids are. They inspired me and gave me strength to keep going. Their smiles were my fuel. I said my love is stronger than my grief. I do not see the sadness or the sickness. I see the joy and the relief my dogs bring to those suffering. That gives me the strength to keep going.

To be honest, I faltered sometimes. I cried when I left the room and walked the empty hallways of the hospital. At that moment I said a prayer for them and for me.

One day my son told me that the mom of one of his friends wanted to send me some stuffed sock toys she made. She loved to sew and that was her therapy. She had many little animal friends made of socks with buttons and ribbons. She knew about my work at the children's hospital and wanted to donate to them. I went to meet her, and we talked about her unique gifts. We became friends and

collaborated with each other. Of course, I said yes! I will take them to the kids. I checked with the hospital, and they gave me the okay.

They became "Mami Prada's Blessings in Socks" it was such a beautiful project. I posted about them and as always, my amazing generous friends wanted to donate materials for my new friend to make more. We collected so many things. It was indeed an incredibly special blessing.

When I visited both children's hospitals, I took a bag with at least ten of them. The kids adored them and were so happy to receive a gift from Mami Prada or Charlie. My friend made a "special edition" and created five little Mami Pradas. Our friends bought them, and we used the money for more materials.

We kept going with visits and shenanigans.

Everyone loved the pictures of our sweet girl Lalique, also known as Cookie, with her parade of hats. She was also the reason I prayed the serenity prayer multiple times.

Lalique is such a special dog. She loved to wear hats, bows, scarves, glasses. She enjoyed our impromptu photoshoots so much.

She was the voice of the page! Many times, I pretended that she made the announcement of something, and everyone took that very seriously. Many responded to her directly. It was a silly game, but our friends loved it! And I did too. That interaction made them happy and looking forward to the next. She was so expressive that it was easy to imagine her thoughts.

Good morning!! ☀️🫶🙆 **Guesssss what????** My mom taking me to see Miss Teresita at The Palace!!! We are going to visit the kids (mom said they are senior kids but kids just the same 😊) that we want to see how I can become a social butterfly and become an awesome therapy doggie! 💮🙆 We will take it slow since I have SOOO much to learn! but I am so excited!!! I need your help! What should I wear? my bandana or my pink bow? Can you tell my mom? Love you! I cannot wait to tell you all about my visit! 😊 🤍 Lalique 💖

They just loved her. She was so precious to all. They did give advice on what to wear. They chose her pink bow.

This is the post about her first observation:

Ohhh Lalique did SOOO well!!! 🤍🐕🙌

There were lots of dogs for the visit. She behaved very well around them. It was a new challenge for her. A new place, dogs, and people. She loved the people!!! She approached them and was not afraid of noise, wheelchairs, or walkers. She did everything I asked her to do. Even followed her mami steps and jumped on the sofas and chairs to get closer to the people. One lady told me she loved her SOOO much! Lali

gave her a lick and she laughed. She said she has not laughed like this in so long. 🐾 that gave me hope that Lali will be amazing. She was a bit distracted by the smells and wanted to wonder. We have a lot to work on. Her focus and walking. As you know she is a little impulsive and wants to take in everything around her! She is a rebel and unique. And I would not change the fur on her head. It is a combination of Prada and Charlie. I cannot wait to help her excel and discover new possibilities as she learns to be her best. Thank you so much for your love and support on her new journey!!! ♡🐕

Cheers and encouragement never faltered. She had her fan club in her paw. We kept the work going and practiced socializing at various places. She slowed down her walk a bit and was more focused.

I got Charlie in trouble.

Well, I got Felix, Gaby, our other library friends, as well as Charlie in trouble. I had the brilliant idea to act out the book we were reading for the book club we created. It was a super cool book. "Dragon Slayers Academy" by Kate Macmullan. I made them costumes. For each of them I made red and blue robes, with gold coins and ribbons. Each had a crown and big spades to slay the dragon — aka Charlie — who had his own dragon costume! They acted out the last chapter with enthusiasm.

We had so much fun! The kids were so kind and without much fuss fulfilled my request.

We had a wonderful time dressing up and recreating the last chapter of the book!!! I made the costumes, and the kids had a blast playing with

Charlie. ♡🐕😊😊😊 he is such a good sport!!! We laughed and had fun during story telling time. It was a total success! Thanks to the moms and Miss Maria, the librarian, for sharing this amazing adventure with us.

Our friends had a good laugh and totally loved our library shenanigans and adventure.

May 2nd, 2018, was Mami Prada's eighth birthday. That week she went to the hospitals with her birthday hat and a little toy cupcake that played the birthday song. She was her best! Somehow, she knew that she was celebrating life!

Ohhhh Mami started her birthday week with a wonderful visit to West Kendall Baptist Hospital!! ♡🙌🎂🐕🐾 The nurses and staff all have so much fun taking pictures with the birthday girl! A couple of kids looked for us so we could visit their mom. It happens they have a golden retriever girl! They loved mami!!! They sang happy birthday and took pictures with her. Then we visited a lady and her husband. We saw her girls by the lobby, and they told us to please visit her. Mami Prada sat on a chair and both the lady, and her husband petted Prada and even figured out that she loves ear scratching ♡ she was so happy! She looked cute in her birthday hat! Lali feels proud of her mami!!! ♡

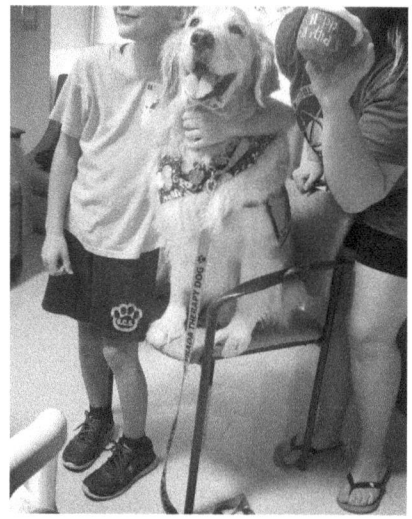

I was fortunate to meet the lady and the kids again at a restaurant nearby. She recognized me and came to see me to tell me how grateful she was that I visited her during her stay at the hospital. She was in love with

Prada and felt so much better after the visit. Her golden was pregnant then. We have become incredibly good friends since.

That night we had a wonderful birthday party for Mami Prada. Ruby and Max came over for cake and fun! They all sat around the table with their birthday hats while the humans sang happy birthday! Mami Prada ate two pieces of vanilla cake! It was her birthday after all. She deserved it and totally enjoyed it.

In July 2018, my sister Maribet and Jack moved to Victoria, Canada. We received a parting gift from her. A yellow amazon parrot named Nina. She is one of the best gifts I have ever gotten. She is funny and clever and has a big attitude. We miss my sister and Jack. We are so happy they are

going to have their own amazing adventure in Canada.

I was very thankful for our Sundays. It was the day for pool parties and sometimes a trip on the boat to the beautiful Keys. It was always the day I would recharge my batteries to keep going for the following week.

Finally, summer arrived, and we packed the car with humans and dogs and off we went to the cabin!

It was so much fun! The dogs were older and more disciplined. They still had selective hearing when I called them back to the cabin. We had tons of adventures. Fresh air and time to rest and recharge. The King of the Mountain was so happy.

My soul was once again replenished with hope and strength. I was always thinking of our future and what would happen. Could I keep up with this routine? I guessed that time would tell.

We were back home ready to go and continue with our lives.

On July 28, Lalique had her second observation for the therapy dog certification.

Lalique passed her second observation with excellence!! 💬🙌🎉 I am so proud of her and how incredibly connected she was with the people. She sat close to them. She even turned her head closer to their lap so they could pet her better. She gave her version of hugs with her paws and totally won everyone's hearts. ♡

It was good to see our sweet French lady and other residents that recognize us.

Lali needs one more visit to complete her test and then become a Therapy Dog. Ohh the places she will go!

We are SOOO excited! I know that she will bring so many adventures to our work! She is a combination of both Mami and Charlie. I cannot wait! 🙌♡🐕 God bless her! She will be a force to reckon with in the Therapy Dog world!

Everyone was waiting for the update! Her fan club was in alert mode. She got cheers and tons of encouragement. She was almost there!

On August 11, 2018, she did it!

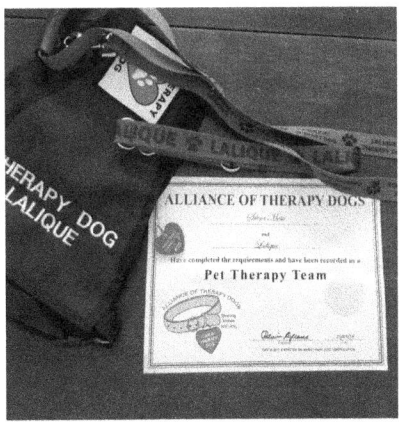

My mom said, "Lalique, you can become whatever you want to be," so I became a THERAPY DOG!! 🙌🐕😊🎉♡ Yey Guys!!! I did it!!!

Lalique is such a loving girl with everyone! I am so proud of her and how she behaves! Now we just need to send in her paperwork and receive her certificate and she will be ready to be part of the team! ♡🐶🦴🐕🐕🐕

We just need to work on walking a little bit less in a hurry. But that's Lali! She does not waste time. Lol.

Thanks so much to all for your love and support!

I cannot wait to see the amazing places she will go! 🐾

How special! Our friends celebrated her milestone with wonderful words of encouragement and love.

We were now a team of four!

Mami Prada, Charlie Brown. Lalique and I. We had so much love for what we did.

On October 12, 2018, we received Lalique's envelope.

Our Journey of Love and Adventure

Helloooo Friends!!!! 🐶🐾 Look what I got!!! My very own Therapy Dog Certificate! 💚✌️🐕🙏 And mom got me my very own collar and leash with my name too!!! I am so happy, and mom is so proud of me! 💚 now she must tell the world and send it to everyone so I can go everywhere like Charlie and Mami Prada!!!! Yey💚✌️🐕😘☺️

Cheers and congratulations messages were amazing! Our funny and beautiful girl was ready to conquer the world!

Lalique did the same as Prada. We visited all the facilities, and she loved all the places we visited. Like Mami Prada, the library was not really her place. She was restless. She wanted to walk around and visit everyone. She loved the kids but loved even more the attention she got from the librarians and patrons. Therefore, I decided her niche would be the adult hospital and the nursing homes.

In October 2018, we had a special visit from our friend Colette and her family. Colette has been a wonderful friend to the Bunch and to me. We met at Lincoln Road in Miami Beach. Needless to say, she enjoyed the company

of Mami Prada, Lalique and Charlie so much. We are so grateful for all her support and love.

I loved our work so much that I wanted to know more. I got books about animal assisted activities and learned a lot about how to understand dog behavior. How can dogs work with kids beyond just visiting them? How can their connection help children at a different level?

I found a wonderful online certification about Human Animal Bond given by Oakland University. I applied and, in a few months, completed it. I was certified as a Human Animal Bond Specialist. I was excited and felt accomplished. I got letters after my name. What about that!

An idea was born in my heart while I was working on the certification. My final paper was about a project that I honestly believed would be the completion of my quest.

Many people wanted to see the dogs again. Unfortunately, most of our visits and the people we meet, beside the elderly at the nursing homes and the nurses at the hospitals, we only saw once.

In my paper I wrote a business plan to create Prada's Bunch Therapy Dog Club House. It was a wonderful place where people could visit with the therapy dogs. We offered different rooms with extraordinary activities. Due to many circumstances, I have not been able to make it happen, yet.

I have no doubt in my mind that one day, I will.

I understand the need and how much benefit dogs bring to people in the community, especially children. It is a dream that I will make happen.

We kept posting about our shenanigans and mischief.

The dogs were older but still very much with a puppy heart. At home they were free. They jumped, barked, and played. When they got their vests on, they were polite and behaved perfectly. They knew how important that was.

Month after month we celebrated our work with posts about our visits. We became known in the community and many schools, universities and other facilities wanted to experience the work we did. We went to many places and spread lots of love and compassion.

During this hectic time, I was worried about our Spiky. He was 13-years-old and started to develop issues with his heart. He was slower and hard to hear. My grumpy little dog was getting old. My heart was sad and dreaded the inevitable.

We went on vacation to Italy the summer of 2019. It was my dream vacation. I spent many years looking forward to it. The day after we returned, our beloved Uncle Spiky passed away. He waited for us to return. He wanted to say goodbye. He was 14-years-old and so much loved by all.

It is with a very heavy heart I share with you that we lost our Uncle Spiky. I am heartbroken as I lost my little boy that was our first family fur kid. I spent all night with him in my arms trying to comfort him. This morning he was in my arms facing me and I asked him what he would like me to do. And he made a devastating decision for me. He passed away with us before I was going to take him to the vet. We are all so sad. He was my kids' first dog, Prada's best friend

and the kids' best uncle. I am so thankful he waited for us to go to heaven. The Bunch's pictures will never be the same. But I know he will always be remembered with love and a smile.

Thank you all so much for your prayers. For your comfort. For loving him and us. ♡🐶🙏

Hundreds and hundreds of messages. They were devastated as were we. He was so cherished and loved. Prayers and words of comfort were pouring out for our family.

My heart was broken. The dogs were sad and knew that something was very wrong.

I received his ashes and paw print after a few days. I had to write a note to my grumpy boy.

Our Journey of Love and Adventure

I have you home now. I promise I will take you to the mountains where you loved to be free and happy. ♡🐶⛰

It has been a week since you went to Doggie Heaven. I deeply miss our routines. Your warmth next to me watching TV or your body pressed to the back of my legs when I sleep. Feeding you at the kitchen counter. Giving you pieces of chicken to trick you into eating your food. Your little walks at night. Looking for you when I open the door when I got home from work. Your impatient bark when I left you downstairs even for a second. Your grumpy face after a bath and your handsome face when you got your haircut after your hippie looks.

You were small. But you took a huge space in our lives. Hundreds of friends miss you and love you like you were theirs.

We will never forget you gave Cristina a chance to love dogs and not be afraid of them. You were my kid.

Thanks, Spiky, for all you did for us in your own way. ♡

Thank you to all our dear friends who have sent messages, cards, and gifts, all in memory of our little by mighty Uncle Spiky. I am forever grateful to have your love and support.

May we remember Spiky in an incredibly unique way. ♡

Thank you, Lord, for this blessing covered in fur.

We mourned our dear Spiky for an extraordinarily long time.

That same year we went on vacation to Italy during the summer, we went to the mountain for Christmas. We took Spiky's ashes to his favorite place. He was home.

We, as a family, we gave our farewell to our Spiky. He is home in his beloved mountain. So long dear friend. You are in the place you love the most ♡🐶 you will be forever in our hearts.

Eternal Father, we bring you our grief in the loss of Spiky and ask for courage to bear it. We bring you our thanks for Spiky who lived among us and gave us freely of his love. We commit our friend and companion into your loving hands. Give us eyes to see how your love embraces all creatures and every living thing speaks to us of your love. Amen.

We missed him so much. It was hard for me to take a picture and sometimes I looked for him before I took it. My grumpy boy.

Little did we know that our lives would never be the same. What we were about to experience changed us all.

Our Journey of Love and Adventure

Chapter 17

"Dogs leave pawprints on our hearts."
Unknown

Our Life Will Not be the Same

When we came back from the mountains, we continued our visits.

January 2020 was in full force. Charlie went to Nicklaus Children's Hospital, special schools' visits, and the library; Mami Prada and Lalique went to the Baptist Hospitals and the nursing homes. We were busy and content. We got our routine settled and working. They were so good and always ready to go when I got home from work.

We got a box from another follower full of handmade small frames with an inspirational note inside. She wanted me to give them to the

kids. And we did it with much love. We called them "Infinite Frame of Love."

Lali had an awesome first visit of the year. She wore her Grinch PJs. She looked so cute!

The happiest and most adorable Grinch girl ever visited the Hospital tonight. 🖤🐾 as soon as we got to the floor, one of the nurses took us to a room in the adult area. Lali got on a chair next to this young disabled adult and gave him kisses and handed him her paw. His eyes lit up and he was happy to have this surprise visit. It was incredibly special to see her get closer to him. I think she would have even laid down with him if I had let her.

Then we went to visit the children. So many smiles and love for her! She knows exactly how to make them feel happy and loved. It is impressive to see how focused she is when doing her work. Even when there is pizza around 😬✌️♡ we sure love what we do and everyone we encounter on our journey. We gave an "Infinite Frame of Love" to a boy who is a cancer patient. He and Lali had a wonderful time connecting. He was in his bed,

and she sat in a chair in front of him. Her paw in his hand. Priceless. He had a mask, but you could see in his eyes the light and smile of his soul. Thank you, Lali, for letting me witness this precious moment. I hope you can feel the mutual love as I did. ♡

Her fan club did not disappoint. Tons of "Awe she is so cute!" Well done, Lali! You are the best! So special.

As it was our tradition, every day we posted good mornings full of love and shenanigans. I also posted old pictures and videos from when the dogs were puppies. It was so sweet to remember them as puppies. They were already five years old. Mami Prada was 10 years old. I kept my daily visits post, and we wished them all a good night. Many of our friends mentioned missing Spiky. I missed him so much too.

On Valentine's Day we got all dolled up and made a great post sending love to our friends.

🐕♡HAPPY VALENTINE'S DAY!♡🐕

Today is the day we celebrate LOVE and FRIENDSHIP. We are so grateful to all of you! Our Prada's Bunch family!! Your love and support have been part of our journey since the day we were born! ♡ We Love you all and treasure your friendship!

Many Blessings!! ♡♡♡♡

We received lots of messages of love back. As always, our friends sent to us kindness and genuine thoughts.

Mami Prada got into a system and a routine. She knew exactly what to do. I had no say on her actions. I was just there holding the leash and being her escort.

Mami Prada had a wonderful visit tonight ♡🐕✌ she was walking with a purpose. As soon as she got to the rooms, she gave lots of love

and kisses to the patients. It was special to see. We visited a girl that was not feeling well at all in the PICU. Mami sat in the chair next to the bed and as the girl tried to reach to touch her, she reached out to and gave her a lick on her hand. Her mom was smiling and in awe. We gave her the sweet new blessing the pink bunny ♡ and

our last patient was a young adult. She did not hesitate! She got into bed very carefully (with permission), went to him and got closer. She gave him kisses and made him smile. After a while she turned around and let him pet her back. I said "Ok let's go, mami." And she came down and got closer to his mom, like saying goodbye.

Time to go home with a smile and the satisfaction of a work well done 🙏🐕♡

Charlie was invited to the Nicklaus Children's Golf Tournament at the PGA National Club. He was so handsome with his golf bandana.

Today Charlie had an amazing adventure! ♡🐕🙌 we went to represent the Pet Therapy Teams of Nicklaus Children's Hospital at their tent at the Golf Tournament the Honda Classic. Charlie got the opportunity to meet so many people, playing with kids and adults alike.

We got the chance to explain our job at the hospital and how special it is for the kids when we visit.

We also had the immense pleasure of meeting Barbara Nicklaus. She and her husband Jack Nicklaus are the heads of the Nicklaus Hospital Foundation. A sweet lady with an amazingly compassionate heart. ♡ She was totally smitten with Charlie and despite all the press and people around her took the time to talk to me about our job.

How special! And she even took a picture with Charlie🐕♡

We walked around and everyone offered a kind smile or comment to Charlie. We thanked dad for driving the two hours' drive each way so we could be there. It did not hurt that he is a golfer and had a wonderful time as well😊♡⛳ We are blessed to do this wonderful job and spread the love and peace Charlie gives to all he meets.

Our friends were overly impressed with Charlie's celebrity status. Lots of "Well done!" And "You are awesome!" comments.

And suddenly, the time that changed our lives forever arrived.

Coronavirus arrived in our town.

On March 11, 2020, I decided it was not safe to be at the hospitals or any other facility were people gathered.

> *"It is not the magnitude of our actions but the amount of love that is put into them that matters."*
> **– Mother Teresa**

Due to the current circumstances, we are living in with the Coronavirus, I regret to say that I will need to pause our visits to the hospitals, nursing homes and the library. Until we get a better idea of how this virus can be controlled and treated. Believe me, this is an extremely hard decision, but I am certain that I must think of the safety of the people we visit, my dogs and myself.

There are so many unknown variables with this virus. The elderly population and people with compromised immune systems (for example, people at the hospitals) are more sensible and more likely to get sick with it. I would be devastated if anyone became infected due to our visits. It is exceedingly difficult to control who pets and who touches the dogs. I have no way to confirm if the person is healthy or has been in contact with someone sick. That is our mission. To connect and bring peace and joy by being in close contact.

Something that now is not a good idea.

I am so sorry, but it is a profoundly serious situation, and we need to take extra consideration for everyone involved.

Thankfully, the hospitals and nursing homes understand and are ok with this.

I pray for the safety of everyone and that hopefully that science can find a treatment soon to save many lives. It is really a scary moment we live in now.

Please be safe. Take care of yourself and your family by being proactive and careful.

My heart is heavy with this decision, but I think is the best ♡ 🐕

Everyone was worried. They understood my position. I was devastated. What would happen to us? How could we help? I was so worried for our elderly friends and the nurses. They became very dear to my heart. For us, our families, and our friends. Things were getting bad.

We helped the best way we could. We made videos and signs and posted them on Facebook and Instagram for the nurses.

We teamed up with a group of therapy dogs that belong to an organization I was collaborating with, Heel 2 Heal Therapy Dogs, and we created a poster with the dogs wearing signs sending a message "We are doing our part to flatten the curve."

We posted many messages to encourage our friends to be safe. We kept our post of good morning and good night. I knew that all our friends needed us.

I ask mom…. "Mom… I wonder? Is everyone ok?" ♡mom said "I hope so Cookie. We are praying extremely hard for everyone's safety."

I said "That is good mom! I hope they see our message. I want to ask!" mom said "Ok Cookie. Let us check how our friends are doing!"

Please drop a comment and tell us how you all are doing! ♡🐕🐕🐕♡ LOVE ya! Cookie

We got many comments on this post from all over the world. They were all as worried as we were.

I started to work from home three days a week to minimize contact with other people. We were isolating ourselves. It was hard.

I was worried for my family and my friends. For now, we were okay. But what would happen if this could not be contained? So many questions.

I needed to find a way to at least help virtually. I started to train Charlie to lay down in front of the laptop. That way we could connect with kids and do a virtual reading program through Zoom or Facetime.

We did a Virtual Reading with Charlie♡📚🐕👦 and our friend Mariangela! They both miss each other so we held virtual reading time! ♡🐕👦♡

After Charlie did his Charlie's dance in his

blanket, he was ready to say hi to Mariangela and listen to her! It was so much fun!

If you want reading time or virtual visit with us, let us know! We are here for you and your family! ♡🐕🐕🐕♡

We got a few friends interested, the nursing home directors called us on Facetime and we spoke with a few of our friends. And we also participated in several schools' Zoom classes. It was not as good as the real thing, but it was an incredibly special opportunity to continue our mission.

Charlie was more cooperative when I figured out a way to place the treat on top of the laptop with a clip to keep his attention on the screen. It worked. I was glad he loves his treats so much.

The news on TV was not very cheerful. The world was in chaos. God help us all.

I started to help a friend from the hospital to make cloth masks. I collected fabrics and she sewed them. Many of our friends bought materials for us. We even found a golden retriever fabric that was so nice. Everyone wanted one. It reminded them of Mami Prada.

We kept our birthday posts trying to cheer everyone's spirits. They were grateful for the respite from shocking news everywhere they looked.

Good morning ☀ **we want to send you sunny smiles to warm your heart and soul and give you happy feelings! Hope you get it and smile too!!**♡🐕🐕🐕♡ **happy Friday Friends! We love you!**

They were so grateful to see the dogs' smiles.

We learned about Tik Tok and started to make videos with music that people love, and we got a sizable number of new followers. It was fun to make and post them. I also shared the videos on our page. Another way to lift the spirits.

To receive this email this morning was a blessing. Since we cannot be at the hospital, the hospital put us on the big screen in the Lobby.

♡🐕🐕🐕🙏 **There are nurses and doctors we have met through our visits. What a blessing to know we are loved and remembered.** ♡🙏🐕 **We pray and hope for the best to come and the moment we can come back and bring joy and love to everyone we visit. Thank you #westkendallbaptisthospital for this recognition. We love you and miss you all!** ♥🏥🐕🐕🐕♡

We felt so honored and humbled that we made such a difference in the time we visited that we were considered for this demonstration about heroes of the hospital.

Our morning post was a favorite. It was like waking up to a blessing among the fears.

Our Journey of Love and Adventure

Good morning ☀

"Let no one ever come to you without leaving better and happier. Be the living expression of God's kindness: kindness in your face, kindness in your eyes, kindness in your smile."

Mother Teresa ♡

Be kind and generous with the treats! 🐕🐕🐕 ♡

Happy Friday and we wish you all a wonderful weekend! ♡ ✌ **LOVE you!**

In August 2020, Mami Prada celebrated four years cancer free! We were so blessed she was healthy and with us. She continued to give so much love to many. This time through the screen. With her kids, they made a difference for those that were sick or isolated.

One morning my dad called. My mom was feeling sick. She presented all the symptoms of Covid. We tried all we could to keep her home and try to alleviate her symptoms. But she got worse. Her oxygen level was going down. We had to take her to the hospital. It was horrific. We had to leave her alone since no family or visitors were allowed. We begged to please let at least one of us be there but it was not possible. A few days later, she had to be intubated. We were devastated. One of the hardest days of my life.

To make it even more stressful, my dad and my sister got the virus too. They had to be inside the house until tested negative. Finally, we were allowed to visit mom at the ICU. But not contact, only from outside of the window. To see my mom like that was extremely difficult. She was always radiant and so strong.

I was the only one safe. I did errands for my dad and took him and my sister food and went to visit my mom for 15 min, the allowed time, every day.

I was so sad and devastated. I did not have the heart to say much or post anything extraordinary. I tried. I really tried to keep up. But my heart was not there.

The dogs felt my pain and sadness. They were always with me, but during those months, they were extra close. Mami Prada, especially. She would lay on my lap and lick my hand. I was so tired and defeated. Life was not fair. Our friends did not know my mom was sick. I was not strong enough to show that pain to them. I knew they would be so worried and concerned. I knew I would not have the strength to reply or talk about it. It was too raw.

After a month, they took her out of the ventilator, but she still had trouble breathing. She was transported to the main hospital to the ICU unit. She had to have a tracheotomy. All these tubes made a fistula between her trachea and her esophagus. She could not eat or breathe by herself.

She fought for her life for 11 months. We stopped our lives to take care of her day and night. They let us be with her in her room. One at a time. No visitors other than us. I worked from home all the time to be available to relieve my dad or my sister since we were with her 24 hours.

She loved my dogs with passion. She helped me save them all and Prada was her favorite. I used to show her videos and pictures and told her about all their silliness and mischief. She would smile and say she loved them. You sure did, mom.

I tried to make funny posts or updates on our efforts to help others. But I needed help myself. Thanksgiving came and then Christmas. I was apart from the rest of the family and friends. I needed to stay safe to help my mom. I had moments where I felt so alone and sad. I did not want to talk to or see anyone. It was a struggle to find joy. How could we lose mom? She was the strongest of all of us.

On May 2, 2021, we celebrated Mami Prada's 11th birthday. My friend Gigi made her a beautiful cake. She wore a birthday crown and received so many beautiful birthday messages. This time there was no birthday party. It was just us.

We kept going one day at a time.

But God decided that it was enough suffering. It was time for my mom to rest. On July 12, 2021, mom went to Heaven. I will never forget the deep heart wrenching pain of losing my mom. The most amazing human in my life. The glue of our family and my dad's faithful companion... Indeed, life was not going to be the same... Now we need to be strong for dad.

Dear Friends.... It is with a heavy heart that I share the loss of our beautiful abuela. She loved our Bunch so much! We will miss her so much too.

♡🐾 she was in the hospital for 11 months. We were taking care of her the whole time. But God has his plan and now she is resting

and with our Lord. I am sure Spiky is at her side. ♡ we will miss her hugs and treats and so many things more.

We love you Abuela. You will always be with us ♡ 🐕 🐕 🐕

Their love was extraordinary. The kind words of condolences and sincere concern were palpable. They were mourning with us. With my entire family. It was very emotional, and I would always be grateful for all their amazing support and demonstration of love.

Life was still playing tricks with my emotions and challenging my capacity to deal with it.

Prada started to have issues with her eyes. She had ulcers. Charlie had surgery on his leg for a torn ligament. The process to heal was extensive and I was worried if he was going to walk well again.

My father-in-law was sick and after many years of being on dialysis he passed away as well. It was another extremely tough time for our family. Abu Ode loved the dogs and was always so happy to share his birthday cake with them.

God was truly testing my strength and my ability to survive. To deal with all.

I posted lots of old pictures and their pool parties. That helped a bit and little by little I got to be more present. More active and open. We were still home. Volunteers were not allowed yet in the hospital, libraries, and nursing homes. It was only our life on our Facebook page.

I posted little messages like this to encourage our friends, and yes to give hope to myself too.

Good morning 🌞 *Lord, help me to live this day, quietly, easily. To lean upon Thy great strength, trustfully, restfully. To wait for the unfolding of Thy will, patiently, serenely. To meet others, peacefully, joyously. To face tomorrow, confidently, courageously.*

Francis of Assisi

May your day be blessed beyond your expectations ♡🐾🐾♡

Happy Weekend friends!! We love you!

In October we went to the cabin. It was our last trip to the Mountains we loved so much. Due to unforeseeable circumstances, we had to sell it.

I did not post during the trip. I wanted to be there. Just there. To think about my life and what I need to focus more on. To mourn my mom.

I did make a post when we returned. I posted videos and pictures. Because I knew we all needed to see dogs being happy and carefree. It helped us all heal our heart.

Good morning ☀

We spent a whole week at our Cabin in NC! ♡🐕🐑🐑🐑♡🏠
It was a lot of fun! We played and went in the creeks and ponds!

We are now returning home. Hope you have a wonderful weekend!

As always, our friends enjoyed our mountain adventures. They were happy to see the dogs enjoy and the place felt like home to us. It was also the last trip for Mami Prada.

Good morning ☀

"For beautiful eyes, look for the good in others; for beautiful lips, speak only words of kindness; and for poise, walk with the knowledge that you are never alone." — Audrey Hepburn

Have a wonderful and adventurous weekend, friends! We love you!
♡🐑🐑🐑♡

We endured so much during the past months that I was not able to create a new calendar. The 2021 "Remember When" edition was the last one.

Hello Dear Prada's Bunch Friends.

Many of you are wondering about the 2022 Calendar... Unfortunately, due to my mom's illness and her passing I was not able to take new pictures or make new fun memories worth of a calendar. Covid also restricted us from having our family group pictures. 😊 Therefore we are not going to produce the 2022 calendar. I want to express my humongous gratitude for your support and loyal friendship. ♡From 2017 to 2021 we were able to keep the memories alive of our precious Bunch. We helped different rescues and made lots of children smile when they saw the calendar during our visits.

We love you all so much and we hope you will still be with us during these times. We hope that you keep the calendars as a remembrance of our fun adventures!

Thank you all! We love you always ♡ 🐕 🐕 🐕 ♡

Silvia, Mami Prada and the Bunch

Our friends understood. They promised they would treasure all the ones they got. That they would remember our journey of love and adventure with fondness and love. It was another loss that was hard to accept.

But the next one was potentially the hardest one.

On December 10, 2021, as a good morning post, I wrote this:

Good morning 🌞

"The openness of our hearts and minds can be measured by how wide we draw the circle of what we call family." **Mother Teresa**

May you have a wonderful weekend, friends! ♡🎄

That morning the dogs were very strange. They did not want to take their usual pictures of smiles and mischief. The three of them lay down on the floor. Even their heads were lying flat. There was something going on that I did not understand.

Mami Prada had been sick. She was breathing heavily for no reason. A few days before I took her to see Dr. Vazquez. She did x-rays and with tears in her eyes she told me that she suspected the cancer was back. Now on her lungs. It has spread already. Mami was 11 years old. We gave her different medications and tried different foods since she did not want to eat much.

That night I finally posted that Mami Prada was sick. I could not do it before. I was hurting. I knew everyone was going to be frantic and worried. But I thought then it was not fair. They needed to know. They loved her and I owe that to them. It was important that they knew.

My dear Prada's Bunch friends…. this is a post that I really did not have the heart to make…. but I reflect at this time, and I think you all would like to keep Mami Prada in your thoughts and prayers.

The cancer is back and affecting her respiratory system. She is having an extremely tough time breathing and does not want to eat much. At this time there is not much we can do but help her be comfortable and love her even more.

Mami has been more than a dog. She has been my soul. My friend. My teacher. I love her smile and her kisses. She can tell you everything with her gaze. She has survived so much and gave so much hope to so many. Her work as a therapy dog is remarkable and so precious. She is a light for so many people.

Our Journey of Love and Adventure

I am not sure how long God will let her be with us, but I will cherish every minute of it. Please keep her in your prayers and in your hearts.

Thank you all so much for all your love. I will let you know any updates.

I knew they would be sad and worried. Hundreds of messages. I was devastated and so thankful for the amazing support. I was crying reading their messages.

Mami Prada was next to me on the sofa. She went down to the floor, panting as she lay down. I lay down next to her, petting her head and giving her kisses. I felt a deep pain in my gut. It was time to let her go.

I told her "It is okay Mami, you can rest. I will forever love you." She looked at me, closed her eyes and lay down her head. She passed away in my arms peacefully.

I will never forget her soft fur, her soulful eyes, her smile.

My life was altered in so many ways.

Rest In Peace beautiful Mami Prada ♥🙏

We will never forget your beautiful smile. Give tons of kisses to Abu and Spiky.

They felt the sorrow as I did. Hundreds of messages. Many

said they were crying and were so sorry. Mami Prada was part of their heart. They will never forget her.

"I am not sure exactly what heaven will be like, but I know that when we die and it comes time for God to judge us, he will not ask, 'How many good things have you done in your life?' rather he will ask, 'How much love did you put into what you did?" — Mother Teresa 🤍🙏

Thank you, my friends. Your love and friendship mean the world to me. I appreciate so much your kind thoughts for Mami Prada 🤍🐕 it is so special to feel the love from all of you. She brought us together and forever I will be grateful for all the adventures, shenanigans, challenges, and everything we have shared through the years. What a blessing to know Mami Prada and the Bunch made such an impact on people's lives. Thank you so much 🤍🐕 we shall continue our adventures and special work.

All in memory of Mami Prada 🙏

And we did.

After a few months life opened. People were more at ease with each other and little by little restrictions were lifted.

We were able to feel freer and we started to open our homes and see our family. Enjoy life again with a different lens.

Life was never going to be the same, I did not have Spiky, mom and Mami Prada with me anymore.

But life taught us that love, support, and friendship do exist. That there are still lots of people that care for each other and that would always care for us. That we need to trust and always do our best to fight for our dreams. Be resilient and never let go of what your heart and mind want.

Our Journey of Love and Adventure

"The meaning of life is to find your gift. The purpose of life is to give it away."
— Pablo Picasso

Even after all the sadness, I keep my Faith strong. We come to this world to fulfill a mission. To make a difference and find our purpose. Thanks to this amazing journey of love and adventure I found mine.

Our journey of love and adventure continues with Charlie Brown and Lalique. Mami Prada and Spiky will always be among us. We were blessed to enjoy a beautiful journey together.

Now, how do I heal? And how do I come back to my hectic life?

I had to make changes to take care of myself. I was not aware of the stress I was putting myself through until I was forced to stop. I needed to reconsider my priorities and options.

I still wanted to help with my dogs. In fact, I was even more determined to find the missing parts of what I called my quest.

To be honest, I was not ready to return to the hospital. I had nightmares about beeping monitors, breathing tubes, and the pain my mom suffered in bed for so long. It was selfish of me. I felt if I were not completely committed and well to do it, I knew my dogs would feel my hesitation and pain. And there was the fact that Mami Prada was not there either. She was the one that enjoyed the visits the most. Time will tell.

I still had other options and my two amazing, wonderful dogs. We were ready for new adventures. We are a team of three. Full of love, compassion, and commitment.

Our very own journey of love and adventure continues....

This special drawing was a gift from my friend Rebekah. It was made by the famous cartoonist John Rasmussen.

Chapter 18

"No one appreciates the very special genius of your conversation as a dog does."
Christopher Morley

Labor of Love by Prada's Bunch

Through the years, some of Prada's kids became of service.

Our Calendar for 2020 was called "Labor of Love Edition" and I dedicated a month to each of them. They live with my family.

I am immensely proud of all of them.

These words were spoken by each of my family at that time.

Ruby, Service Dog:

Ruby came into our life when she was a puppy and learned to take care of us since then. She is our special companion. Even though she is my service dog, she also takes care of Papi. She is special to him and loves to cuddle. She learned that her work is to be always near me and has helped me with two falls. She is always looking after us and she knows what we need. She is quiet and likes to sit by my feet under the table or the sofa. We love to go to places and walk with her. Ruby loves people but she knows she is our guardian and never leaves our side. We are so blessed to have the chance to enjoy her company and service. It is incredibly special that Ruby gets to see her family and share with her mom Prada and siblings. We are the grandparents of Prada's Bunch!

Mami and Papi

After my mom passed away, Ruby has been my dad's faithful companion. She represents the love they shared.

Max, Service Dog:

Max came into my life when he was 2-years-old. After a few months of intense love, training and help, Max became a special and happy sensitive dog. When Max and I met we had an immediate connection. We just bonded. We both needed each other in our lives. Max had all the necessary training to become a service dog and he helped me so much. He kept me calm during hospital stays, he helped me stay focused when in crowded places. He really helped me go through the motions of my depression. He was so patient and loving. He knew exactly what to do and when to do it when in distress. He is super smart and an amazing dog. Max saved my life! He is truly my best friend!

Max's Mom, Luly

Lily, Special Companion, and Emotional Support Dog:

My faithful friend, my sweetheart... My puppy girl that I adore so much! Your heart is pure gold! The unconditional love you give every single day not only to me, but to anyone you see is truly incredible... You bring joy to the saddest heart and love to everyone who comes to give you a quick hello! Thank you for your constant companionship, for being my shadow... for helping me

overcome one of the darkest moments that this life has given me... Whenever I feel down, you come with your warm puppy smile, bright and gentle eyes, and soft paws and instantly I am happy again! Our lives are incredible because you are a part of it! Every doggie kiss, paw lift, tail wag and boop nose from you make my heart melt! Our conversations are based on sounds, but we understand each other even if others do not! You have listened to countless stories and seen many of my tears... Your love and support are always with me.

Mami LuLu

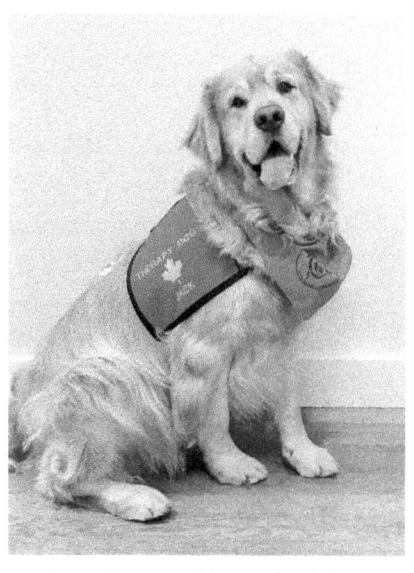

Jack, Therapy Dog:

Outgoing, friendly, mischievous, and full of energy but so loving and empathetic, Jack stole our hearts right away. He did his Good Canine Citizen training and passed with excellence! Once we moved to Canada, he became a certified Therapy Dog with the Pacific Animal Therapy Society. Jack gets extremely excited when we arrive at the BC Cancer Center where he loves to shake his paw, sit on his hind legs, and give hugs and kisses for delicious treats! We are also a R.E.A.D. Team at South Park Elementary School and are part of The Pet Café at the University of Victoria where he gets so pampered by the students. Jack also visits nursing homes and shares one-on-one. In his free time his most favorite activities are swimming, playing with his tennis balls and chasing the squirrels on the deck. Jack is also my partner in my journey as an advocate for healthy baking. He is the Sous-Chef of my kitchen and the expert in healthy dog treats.

Mom Maribet and Dad Gary

Charlie Brown and Lalique came to be the social butterflies of the Bunch. Being therapy dogs, they had a different mission with their unique love for what they do. They are also my own emotional and the most incredible support I could ever have.

God blessed us with an incredibly special and unique Bunch.

On January 1, 2022, we celebrated the Bunch's seventh birthday. Charlie and Lalique represented their siblings.

Happy Birthday Charlie, Lali, and the Bunch 🎂💞🎂 YOU are the best Birthday kids ever!! 😆♡🎂🎂 those cupcakes were sooo delicious!

Our friends sent lots of love and happy birthday wishes. Our birthday table was not the same, Mami Prada was not with us this time. She loved cake so much I did not have the heart to get one. We got cupcakes for the kids.

I tried my best to keep up with our happy Friday posts which now included pictures of our new family members. The Bunch of the Porch.

My mom sent me new souls to take care of to keep my heart busy. She loved cats. My neighbor, Cristina, cares for some of the cats by our houses. I wanted to help her and placed a bowl of cat food on my porch.

And just like that, I got my own cat sanctuary on my porch.

My first cat was Papa. He was living across the street at my friend Cristina's house. One of her cats had kittens and he was not fond of those annoying little things and came to live on my porch. Then I got four other residents, Willow, Oliver, Eleonor, and Millie, plus the occasional raccoons. Oliver came the week my mom passed away. It was definitely her doing.

One of the cats, the tuxedo one who I

named Oliver, decided that he wanted to be an inside cat and live the best life. He loved to get inside when I opened the door. He would stay hidden all day and let me know it was time to go outside and go on his own adventure at night. Eventually he stayed inside the whole time.

Oliver is a blessing to my soul. Oliver and Nina, my yellow amazon parrot, were also great emotional friends during my mourning period. Somehow Nina learned to say Prada. One day after Prada passed away, she said it. And now I am Prada to her. When I get out of her sight, she screams Prada! I wonder if she feels Mami Prada is still with us. Nina is also part of our Friday morning hellos!

Good morning 🌞

Love is patient and kind; love does not envy or boast; it is not arrogant or rude. It does not insist on its own way; it is not irritable or resentful; it does not rejoice at wrongdoing but rejoices with the truth. **Corinthians 13:4–8a**

Love is a kind face with four paws and a friend with green feathers. ♡

We hope you have a wonderful weekend! May you see and feel love and kindness around you always!

We love you! ♡ 🐾 🐾 ♡

Our friends welcomed our new additions. Everyone had a kind word for the cats and Nina was a favorite one of many with her big attitude and precious yellow and green feathers.

In February 2022, we received an email from a local high school asking us to come to do a presentation in one of their after-school clubs. I was nervous and happy! This is what I needed.

I created a PowerPoint presentation about Charlie's journey and off we went. Charlie was amazing! It was like he never missed a beat. He walked around the kids and accepted their love as good as he gave.

It was a blessing. We were back!

I do my best when I am busy. And this was my sign that I needed to step up and keep on going with my dreams.

The library started our program again and we were welcomed with lots of love.

Charlie Brown had a blast today at the South Miami Library ♡📚🐶 **we had a nice group of kids. One of the kids read a book called Charlie B.** 👍🐶 **a special book about a pup like Charlie that wanted to be a therapy dog. The funny thing is that his mom had short blond hair like me! the kids thought it was me!**

One of the kids used Charlie's paw to follow the line 😁 (poor Charlie is indeed in need of a pawdicure!) usually Charlie is not fan of people taking his paw for a while, but he understood his assignment and was calm and went along with the plan 😊👋.

After the books, we played Lego with the little one and Charlie did his tricks for cookies, of course. And then his famous Charlie's

 dance in the library carpet (he loves to scratch his back on the carpet) when we were done. It is so good to see how he responds to the kids, his calm demeanor. That is an exceptional quality. ♡🙏🐕 we really enjoy our time together and helping the kids! ♡

Our friends were so excited to see us coming back to what we love! Lots of "Well done Charlie!" "You are the best!" "Awesome!"

We had a wonderful visit from one of our Prada's Bunch friends. Amy came to Florida to visit her dad. She wanted to meet us and of course we welcomed her with so much love. To have Amy home was special.

 **Today we got a wonderful visit! Our friend Amy came over to meet us all from Chicago! It is such a beautiful moment to meet someone that "we know" and have shared so many moments. Good and bad. We had a delicious lunch with some Cuban pastries that she never tried before. ♡😊 the dogs loved her! It was so funny to see her reaction when she recognized our home from all the pictures! I am thankful for your friendship Amy. Come back soon! ♡ we love you!**

The mischiefs and shenanigans were still part of our lives. Now included a "Black fur ball" also known as Oliver, the cat.

Picture this: Lali saw Oli under the table and was focused. I saw her and then saw Oli. I figured out her intentions. I opened the door to give Oli an escape route 👍 and off he went. And Lali after him. Running. Like chasing with purpose so I ran after them! Passed the driveway and then Oli crossed the street. Thankfully, Lali stopped when I told her and came back into the driveway. Meanwhile.... Charlie Brown was having a feast of cat food on the Porch and watching the whole spectacle 😆. I got Lali inside. And when I was about to close the door, can you believe Oli came back in? Oh dear. Never a dull moment ♡ 🐈 ⬛ 🐕

One of the funniest comments was:

"A typical day at the Mesa house" Ha! They know us so well!

Lalique and Oliver learned to live together and now they are friends.

Lalique also had a special school visit. Since the nursing homes were still closed to volunteers, I did not want Lalique to lack confidence in her job and going for a visit was going to be good for her. I took her to this high school that she had visited before.

Lalique made a wonderful comeback at Terra Environmental School! 🐾 📚 🐕 the high school kids were in love with her and asked lots of questions about our journey and all the steps to make it. ♡👍 Lali did good. She was a bit nervous and excited about all that was going on. This is her

second time visiting the school. She even has a school ID! 🐕🙏👍📚♡ excellent job Lali!

Her fan club was all in attendance. The post went viral and there were tons of happy comments. They were so excited and pleased that Lalique did such a wonderful job! They all felt so proud of her!

And like that, day by day, we came back to doing what we love. Bringing love, hope, companionship, empathy, and sometimes stillness.

The dogs are getting old. They are now eight years old. Their faces have white fur and sometimes they are not as active as before.

It makes my heart a bit nostalgic. I enjoy them, give them tons of kisses and cuddles and I am blessed to hear their snores next to me while I write our journey.

They are amazing and so loved by hundreds of people around the world and especially by their family.

Our journey with Prada and the Bunch was incredibly special. We learned to love each other and many strangers that became family. We received so much support and kindness. We discovered the power of prayer and unconditional love.

Gratitude is one of the most rewarding feelings we as human beings can experience. It is simply amazing. It makes you feel content and humble.

I am so grateful for all the difficulties of life that taught me to be humble. For all the disappointments and successes. For the journey God gave me to follow.

I am grateful every day for all the blessings I have. Especially for my family. For Miguel, my beautiful kids, for my parents, my siblings, my friends, for my dogs, cats, and parrots.

I am grateful for the work I do with my dogs as I have learned to open my heart to many people we encounter. Some we see again. Some we will never see again.

I am grateful that we bring love and much comfort.

I am grateful that I have dreams. That I have goals. That one day I will fulfill them all.

I have learned to be a better human because of the love of my dogs.

I thank my angels that protect me and guide me. I thank God for my life and my blessings.

I am grateful for so many amazing friends, for You, Prada's Bunch and Friends, that encouraged me and loved my dogs through eight amazing years.

I am grateful to have had Prada in my life.

Our Journey of Love and Adventure

I am grateful you came along to walk with us.

'I am a little pencil in the hand of a writing God, who is sending a love letter to the world' Mother Teresa

The End

Epilogue

"A dog is the only thing that can mend a crack in your broken heart."
Judy Desmond

Having the opportunity to make a difference in someone's life is truly a blessing. Sometimes we do not realize that a small gesture of kindness can be the thing that the other person needs the most.

I have learned a lot about how humans and dogs interact. The special connection that forms and brings out the best of them both.

I love how people look into the eyes of my dogs and find peace. I love how they rejoice by just softly petting their fur. You cannot imagine the transformation that a person goes through in the minutes they see the dogs and spend time with them. Sadness and fears become happiness and hope. I remember Prada walking in the hospital and the air changing. The smiles flow like her beautiful tail. That is genuine love. No conditions, no expectations. Just pure and genuine love.

I found my purpose thanks to my dogs and all the events and people I encountered.

I found that working with Charlie at the library and at the psychiatric ward at the children's hospital gave me so much joy that I decided to channel my purpose on helping kids. Our society is difficult to navigate, and children now more than ever need us to guide them and provide them with unconditional love.

I want to make a difference for the kids, and I see how they respond when Charlie is with them. Even the tougher ones lower their guards and simply accept Charlie's love.

I researched and studied many options to make this a reality. I found a wonderful life coaching for kids' program called Adventure in Wisdom that inspired me and opened the door to what I was looking for.

I completed the certification and now Charlie and I work together helping kids be better humans and kinder to themselves and others. My purpose was a vision. And I am making it happen. I created my life coach for kids' business, Charlie's Wags of Wisdom. Together we give kids tools to navigate life in a positive and sympathetic way.

I love to help others understand this beautiful work of dog therapy. I also volunteer and work with a wonderful organization called Heel 2 Heal Therapy Dogs. Together we help new teams find places to share the love of their four-legged friends. I help guide the new teams and share my experiences to make it easier for them to volunteer.

Being a therapy dog team gives humans the chance to connect on another level with a dog. It is important to learn how the dog behaves and why. Our priority is our dog. Making sure they are happy doing this job is important. We are a team. And that is how we share our love with the world.

I love to visit the nursing homes with Lalique and Charlie. Our work there is so special and meaningful as well. We bring joy and light to many that are forgotten. We go the extra mile to make them feel love. Their smiles are priceless. Their fragile hands tell a story. Their lost gaze shows their pain. I have met many of them who have become dear to my heart. I have mourned for some who have passed away. I cherish their life and honor their love. Sharing my dogs with them is special.

While I was working on Human-Animal Interventions certification, I had an incredibly special vision.

I wish to open a facility where people can visit therapy dogs. I would call it Prada's Bunch Therapy Dog Club House. What a wonderful place to be! When we visit hospitals or schools, we always get so much love, and we get asked how they can meet Charlie or Lalique again? This place of mine would give them that chance. Can you imagine this special place where adults and kids come to visit and spend time with well trained and kind therapy dogs? How special is that!

This facility would also serve as a training site for new teams. There are a lot of vital details that need to be learned to excel as therapy dog teams. I want to share what I know in a more professional way. I know one day; my vision will have a home.

I volunteer with Charlie Brown at four libraries on Saturdays. I have made significant improvement in the way we reach children and how to keep them interested in reading. We keep working at Nicklaus Children Hospital psychiatric ward. Helping the kids feel better and happy. We visit schools and talk about our work in the community.

Lalique and I go to the nursing homes on Sunday visiting the young at heart. We play games with them and bring lots of different activities. During the holidays we take pictures with Lalique, and we bring them the picture for keepsake. They love it. Charlie also visits and they adore him.

I now enjoy weekday evenings at home with my family and I work on many projects. I learned to find a balance that benefits myself and those around me.

I still have my dear Prada's Bunch and Friends Facebook page up and running. We post our Friday hellos and I keep posting our visits. Many of the original followers are still with us after eight years.

My dear and amazing friends. I cannot thank you enough for the love you give me and my dogs and how blessed I am to have you all as part of our family.

If you just met us, I invite you to visit us and be part of our beautiful community.

Thank you for coming with us during this special journey of love and adventure. I am forever grateful.

I cannot wait to see what the future holds for my purpose. I love it now and I am sure it will be amazing then.

See you at our next adventure....

Acknowledgements

*"For the yesterdays and todays,
and the tomorrows I can hardly wait for
– **Thank you."** Cecelia Ahern*

I would like to express my gratitude to my husband Miguel for always supporting unconditionally my crazy ideas and adventures. For being the calm to my storm. Thank you for celebrating all the exciting moments of my life with me. I cannot imagine not having you by my side for every magical experience.

My children Cristina and Carlos. You make me proud. I am a better person and mom because of you. Thank you for loving me even when I am annoying. This book is one of my dreams come true. Both of you and dad inspired me and gave me courage to make it happen.

Thank you to my dear Charlie Brown and Lalique. I cherish you and will do anything to keep you safe and always loved. I am honored to work by your side and make a difference in so many people's lives. And my angels Spiky and Prada. My original kids. Forever grateful for your love.

I want to thank my amazing mom in Heaven. She always knew with a look what I had on my mind. She believed in me and was so proud of my work and my journey. She adored Prada and I know she is so proud of me for authoring this beautiful book. Thank you, mom, for your love and devotion. I love you and miss you. Keep watching over all of us.

I want to thank my dad for his love and wonderful guidance. For his steady presence and support. His kindness and generosity have been a wonderful example to me and that paved the way I carry my life with integrity and compassion. Thank you, Papi. I am grateful to be by your side.

Thank you Aya and Abu Ode in Heaven for loving me as your daughter. For loving my dogs even though you prefer cats.

Thank you to my sisters Maribet, Luly, Dannia and Olga and my brothers Tony, Beto, and Leo and all my nieces and nephews. You all make our family special.

Thank you, Miguel, Maribet, Gary, and Cari for reading my manuscript and helping me make sure I was not making a mess of my emotions.

Thank you to my wonderful editor, Maddie. I appreciate so much your help in understanding my thoughts and enhancing this wonderful manuscript.

Thank you, my dear Prada's Bunch and Friends Facebook family. I would not have gotten here without you. I am so grateful for the opportunity to share our journey and being able to connect with all of you. Your support was unconditional. Even though I have never met you in person, except for a few, I consider you all my friends. Thank you to everyone that one way or another helped me fulfill my dream.

Thank you to my friends on Facebook and in life. I appreciate your support and being so patient with all my posts about my dogs. For stepping up when I need you. I am glad we connect and support each other.

Thank you to all the people who I have met during my work with the dogs as therapy dog teams. You make me smile, cry, and fight for my dreams. Thank you to the children that I meet every visit that fill my heart with so much love and joy. You inspire me.

Thank you to Rikki, Natasa and Stuart and all the staff of Ultimate 48 hours authors for showing up in my life and encouraging me into this endeavor. It was a pleasure to meet Nat and Stu in person. You made me feel special and capable of making one of my dreams come true. Your guidance and mentoring are amazing.

And always I thank you God and my angels for guiding my thoughts and my actions to make this journey a memorable one. For bringing Prada into my life and giving me the strength to move on and find my purpose.

Further Testimonials

"Once someone has had the good fortune to share a true love affair with a Golden Retriever, one's life and one's outlook is never quite the same."
Betty White

Prada is the reason I fell in love with golden. Her love for everyone was so clear in her face, the way her eyes seemed to shine at you, and in her smile. Her babies are all equally amazing, particularly their acts of service with their human Mama Silvia. They are mischievous, love to swim, sweet and loving and tend to still think they are lap dogs. Mami Prada loved her tennis balls.

Jane Davis
Harrisonville, Missouri

I have known Silvia and her beautiful bunch ever since I became a member of the Facebook group 'Golden Retriever Owners and Lovers' eight years back! I have seen and been inspired by her journey with mami Prada and Uncle Spiky to the adorable Prada's Bunch. They inspired Coffee and me to start our journey as an extended family. Silvia and Prada guided us to step into motherhood and share the joys of being surrounded by wonderful golden kids. Despite the geographical distance between us, Silvia, Prada, Uncle Spiky and the Bunch have been inspiring us and brightening our days. Their love and dedication have inspired many more than just me. Though we have never met physically, I have felt the joy, the pain, and the love with each of Silvia's posts.

**Shivani Barthwal & Coffee,
Dehradun, Uttarakhand, India**

What Prada's Bunch means to us is something akin to a precious memory, one that will stay with us for the rest of our lives. Prada taught us to never give up in the face of any adversity that comes our way. We will always remember when we had the opportunity to visit Prada and how it filled us with the love that only she could provide. Prada will always be in our hearts and will always be remembered for her never-ending kindness and love for everyone.

**Natalia, Olivia, Valeria, Dania & Javier
Miami, Florida**

Silvia's love for Prada and all her pups will truly melt your heart, as it did mine. Prada's Bunch is full of love, adventure, laughter, and tears. I had the pleasure of meeting Prada, and totally fell in love with her sweet soul. Silvia certainly captivates her audience with Prada's heartwarming journey.

**Colette Broeckel
Gardner, Massachusetts**

I stepped into Silvia and Charlie Brown's life because of a mutual teacher friend. I would see her posts online and see how wonderful and beneficial their work was to the community. Sometimes, in life it is the trivial things that you do every day that build big and magnificent accomplishments. Charlie Brown and Silvia bring with them peace, love, joy, and calmness. Charlie Brown's smile melts our students' hearts in many ways, and they can form a connection for a specific moment built on trust, kindness, and empathy. Unknowingly, Charlie Brown and Silvia bring these experiences to the students I serve who are a very vulnerable and fragile population within the school. Their visits are welcomed by all, including our faculty, staff, but most of all our students. Thank you, Silvia, and Charlie Brown, for sharing this journey of love that you share through your work of service to the community!

Annette P. Zayas
Miami, Florida

Prada's Brunch changed lives by sharing an abundance of compassion, comfort, and joy to the patients and staff at West Kendall Baptist Hospital. The instant you saw them coming your way, your day was better! I am forever grateful for their outstanding service!

Cindy Hovde
Volunteer Director West Kendall Baptist Hospital
Miami, Florida

When I read Prada's Bunch postings I am always smiling and feeling lighter at the end. I experience a lot of physical pain daily; Prada's postings make my day happier.

Morgan and Cosmos
Church Creek, Maryland

Mami Prada's life was filled with many surprises and her legacy continues to be a gift for those who encounter her precious BUNCH. This story must be retold – heartwarming is the faithfulness between Mama Silvia and the sweetness overload of Mami Prada and her babies. Just sit back, sip on a warm cup of café con leche and a croqueta or two (Charlie's favorite delicacy) as you engage in this beautiful inspiring story.

Caridad Roque
Teacher
Miami, Florida

Me and wife have followed Prada, and her pups, Charlie and Lalique since the beginning of their journey. Initially because we love golden retrievers, but we must come to realize they are more than just that! Silvia, their owner, through her training has worked with them to become therapy dogs, visiting local care homes, hospitals, and libraries, and sharing their love with people of all ages. The joy they bring not only brings joy to those they visit but also those who follow them.

I have only just touched the tip of the iceberg of their incredible journey which I am sure will be a long and happy one!

Stephen Parker
Weston, U.K.

This is an amazing tribute to Prada. I am honoured to have been a part of Prada's journey. I cannot imagine the depth of your loss of Prada. It was clear when I met you, how much love you had for her. She was so fortunate to have had the love, support, and care of your family. Prada was surrounded by prayer and love. It was truly your care that carried her for all those years.

Lisa DiBernardi, DVM
Prada's Oncologist
Houston, Texas

Our Journey of Love and Adventure

I stumbled across Prada's Bunch one day on Facebook merely by accident, and I have been following since, anxiously waiting to see what each day brought. Watching them on all their adventures — be it local on a day trip to the beach, a birthday celebration where the only question is — will they wait for everyone else before getting into the cake, or a family vacation to the mountains, they put a smile on your face each and every day.

From Prada's work as a mother, although she would often lead them astray on an unauthorized trip to the swimming pool, to big, loveable Charlie's growth into an amazing therapy dog. And then there's Lalique, that sweet girl who will most likely have the roll of toilet paper if you cannot find it, but she will give you one of those special little head tilts, and all is well! Love them all!

Michael Rogers
Shawnee, Kansas

It was one of those times when you are sad, depressed, and down. I had just had an emergency surgery where sadly I lost my last good ovary, sending me into an abrupt menopause and on a roller coaster of emotions. Laying on a hospital bed, missing my kids and my dogs, suddenly a knock on the door changed my day. "Come in," I said. And there was beautiful Prada and her handler, who later I learned was Silvia Mesa.

They came in and filled my room with a such a positive vibe and love that I forgot all about my symptoms. See, I have a golden retriever girl as well, her name is Roberta, and I was dying to see her. Somehow Prada filled her shoes and with her sweet noble face and smiles, she changed my days in the hospital for the better.

I thanked Silvia a lot for coming over, it really made a huge impact on me and my stay in the hospital. A few months later while leaving a restaurant, I saw a handsome gorgeous golden retriever boy at the door picking up To Go food with a beautiful lady and as I got closer, it was my Angel from the hospital, Silvia Mesa. I asked where is Prada and who is this handsome boy? That is how I met Charlie Brown and that is how my friendship with Silvia started. We not only have the exact same name, but we also share the same love and passion for dogs, especially golden retrievers.

Silvia and I have been through some rough times together, from losing family members like a mother, and my brother, but the connection we have with the dogs always made our souls feel better.

I loved late dinners at her house while on shift (I am a police officer) and patrol Silvia's area. She spoiled me with delicious midnight treats and of course visiting Prada, Charlie and Lalique back then made my long night shifts much better.

I will forever be so thankful to God for sending me such a sweet, loving and thoughtful person into my life, thank you Silvia for your friendship, for your work and dedication with your dogs and the community impact you make every day with them. I know there's people with stories like mine, people who you had visited in the hospital and had created memories like you did with me.

Love you my friend, I pray God blesses you and your family and your four-legged children in all you do. Blessings.

Silvia Nadal
Miami, Florida

Silvia, you are amazing. You have touched more lives in more ways than you will ever comprehend. I have followed your journey as you fulfill your dreams, which I feel was purely for the sake of others. I could feel your warmth, happiness, and heartache from all which you have chosen to share.

The involvement of the human and furry kids' Abuela, your mom, was so significant in your journey to who you are today. Keep embracing and enjoying all that you do. I honestly believe she, Prada and Spiky are watching from above in the "party in the sky."

Your mom was my idol! She just jumped in and both of you worked so great as a team. She is missed from afar. My heart still hurts for your broken one. I will forever be a "fan" of you. I remember you reaching out on Facebook for advice and guidance when you felt you needed it, while Prada was delivering. That is when I first thought you were a wonderful, honest person. As my son and I would refer to someone like you, "they are the real deal!"

Wishing you much joy of the success of your journey! I look forward to reading your book.

Carol Hyman Connel
Westwood, New Jersey

Prada's Bunch fun fact:

✉️I went to take a box to the post office. I made a friend at the post office who has helped me with the tons of envelopes and packages I have sent since I started selling cards, etc.

He asked me what I was sending this time. So, I gave him a small summary. He interrupted me and said "I know! You need to write a book! 🐾You need to write about everything you have done and what Prada survived!!" So darling♡ He surely was incredibly positive about that.

Then he said, "Oh, I always wondered how you always kept your house so nice and clean?" I said, "Wait what? Do you see my posts?" And he said, "Well I am Facebook dumb, but I have a friend. I asked her to go in and look for your page and see Prada's Bunch!" Lol ♡😁 What do you know? Our dear post office friend is one devoted fan of the Bunch! 😊🐾📬✉️

These testimonials are based on each person's experience with Prada's Bunch and Friends Facebook page and real-life encounters.

About The Author

Silvia Mesa was born in Barquisimeto, Venezuela on March 9, 1970. She lived with her Cuban parents Antonio and Lourdes Balestena and her siblings Maribet, Luly, Tony and Beto until 1989 when the family and her two Pekinese dogs decided to move to Miami, Florida seeking a better life.

In 1995, Silvia got married to Miguel Mesa and had two children, Cristina and Carlos. Silvia graduated from FIU in 1998 with a bachelor's degree in business administration. She currently works as an administrator for her dad's real estate company. In 2017 she became a therapy dog handler and teamed up with her golden retrievers Prada, Charlie Brown and Lalique.

Silvia loved her work as a therapy dog team so much that she got a certification from Oakland University in Human-Animal Interventions.

After six years working as a volunteer in libraries with her therapy dog Charlie Brown, Silvia decided to look for a certification that could facilitate her to work with children. In January of 2023 she obtained a certification from Adventure in Wisdom, a program that helps kids with their mindset skills. Silvia is also now a Life Coach for Kids with her partner therapy dog Charlie Brown. Together they run Charlie's Wags of Wisdom.

Silvia is currently living in Miami, Florida with her husband Miguel, her children Cristina and Carlos, her two golden retrievers Charlie Brown and Lalique, her indoor cat Oliver and her feathery kids Nina, a yellow amazon parrot, and Cuchi, a quaker parrot. Silvia is also a caretaker of three outdoor cats that live on her front porch. Willow, Millie, and Eleonor, and a few others including the occasional raccoon family. She is a big animal lover.

Walking with Prada is her first book.

Contact information and social media:
Email pradasbunch@gmail.com
Facebook: Prada's Bunch and Friends
Instagram: @pradasbunchandfriends

Speaker Bio

"Walking with Prada"

Silvia Mesa is the author of *Walking with Prada*, a beautiful memoir that encompasses the life of her family and her beloved dogs.

Silvia graduated from Florida International University in 1998 and currently works as a business administrator. An immigrant from Venezuela, Silvia and her family achieved the American dream by becoming US citizens a few years after arriving in Miami, Florida. In 1995, Silvia married her husband, Miguel Mesa, and together they created a beautiful family. They have two children, Cristina and Carlos. She also lives with her two golden retrievers, Charlie Brown and Lalique, and a few other furry and feathery friends.

In 2017, Silvia became certified as a therapy dog handler and teamed up with her golden retrievers Prada, Charlie Brown and Lalique. Sadly, Prada passed away from cancer in 2021. Silvia currently visits libraries, hospitals, schools, and nursing homes with Charlie Brown and Lalique. She loved her work as a therapy dog team so much that she obtained a certification from Oakland University in Human-Animal Bond Intervention. After six years working as a volunteer with her therapy dog Charlie Brown, Silvia decided to look for a certification that could facilitate her to work with children. In January of 2023 she obtained a certification from Adventure in Wisdom, a program that helps kids with their mindset skills. Silvia is now a Life Coach for Kids with her partner in crime, Charlie Brown. Together they run Charlie's Wags of Wisdom.

Through the years, Silvia has encountered several opportunities to help others learn about the wonderful job that is volunteering as a therapy dog team. Her certification in Human-Animal Bond Intervention gives her the opportunity to educate others on the differences between Animal Assisted Activities, Animal Assisted Education, and Animal Assisted Therapy as well as how to setup a program to achieve desired outcomes.

The experiences Silvia had through her work as a handler of three loving therapy dogs gave her an understanding of working with human and dogs at the same time. Training, temperament, and compassion is fundamental for the job. She has mastered many ways to work with people at hospitals, nursing homes, schools, libraries, and many other facilities.

Silvia has since channelled her work towards helping children. Through her business, Charlie's Wags of Wisdom, Silvia, and Charlie Brown have created group workshops and they also can work with kids one-on-one to find tools that help them navigate the difficult and amazing moments that life has to offer.

As an engaging, inspiring, and approachable speaker, Silvia Mesa brings to life her passions that she has gained through many years of experience.

HOW TO BE THE BEST THERAPY DOG TEAM

- Recognizing the potential in your dog and yourself in order to give love to strangers.

- How to navigate training and become a talented team player with your dog.
- Finding love and passion in volunteering.

HOW TO APPROACH THE OPPORTUNITIES TO WORK WITH YOUR SPECIAL BEST FRIEND

- Learning to understand the connection between you and your dog and the special bond you get through volunteering.
- Learning where the best place to volunteer is and how to connect with them.
- Finding the positive aspect of including your therapy dog to help advance your career.

HOW TO HELP CHILDREN APPROACH LIFE IN A POSITIVE WAY - WITH CHARLIE BROWN, THERAPY DOG - CHARLIE'S WAGS OF WISDOM

- Empowering kids through stories and Charlie's Wags of Wisdom to help develop mindset skills.
- Identify and shift limiting beliefs that hold kids back.
- Learning to work with activities like storytelling, games, and arts and crafts enables kids to connect to their own thoughts and feelings.

To contact Silvia Mesa please email her or connect with her through her social media channels, listed below:

Pradasbunch@gmail.com
Facebook page: Prada's Bunch and Friends
Instagram: @pradasbunchandfriends

www.ingramcontent.com/pod-product-compliance
Lightning Source LLC
Chambersburg PA
CBHW041315110526
44591CB00021B/2796